Financing Small
Business in America

FINANCING SMALL BUSINESS IN AMERICA

Debt Capital in a Global Economy

Roger E. Hamlin and Thomas S. Lyons

Westport, Connecticut
London

Library of Congress Cataloging-in-Publication Data

Hamlin, Roger E.
    Financing small business in America : debt capital in a global economy / Roger E.
Hamlin and Thomas S. Lyons.
        p. cm.
    Includes bibliographical references and index.
    ISBN 0–275–97673–4 (alk. paper)
    1. Small business—United States—Finance. 2. Credit—United States. I. Lyons, Thomas
    S. II. Title.
HG4027.7.H35 2003
338.6′42—dc22   2003059651

British Library Cataloguing in Publication Data is available.

Library of Congress Catalog Card Number: 2003059651
ISBN: 0–275–97673–4

First published in 2003

Praeger Publishers, 88 Post Road West, Westport, CT 06881
An imprint of Greenwood Publishing Group, Inc.
www.praeger.com

Printed in the United States of America

The paper used in this book complies with the
Permanent Paper Standard issued by the National
Information Standards Organization (Z39.48–1984).

10 9 8 7 6 5 4 3 2 1

CONTENTS

ILLUSTRATIONS

TABLES

FIGURE

INTRODUCTION

This book concerns itself with a form of public/private partnership—the provision of debt capital to small businesses. This topic is important because of the consequential role that such businesses have played, and continue to play, in the viability of the U.S. economy. Unlike larger companies, small businesses often lack the financial capital they need to sustain their growth and development. This is exacerbated by the vicissitudes of economic globalization. Most policy makers view this latter fact, coupled with the economic importance of these small firms, to warrant public intervention in the capital market.

Yet, how much thought is given to the challenges presented to small business by the global economy, and what those challenges imply, both for small firms and for public efforts to assist them? This chapter explores this question by first establishing a working definition of "small business" and by examining the roles, past and present, that small companies play in the U.S. economy. It then enumerates the major challenges afforded by economic globalization and discusses what they mean for enterprise development in America. Finally, it brings the discussion back to the focus of this book—the public role in small business debt capital assistance.

In Chapter 2, small business capital formation is discussed in regard to enterprise development, with an emphasis on small business's place in the larger financial intermediary system. Types, styles, sources, and risk levels of debt capital are explored. In particular, the theoretical foundation for government's role in small business, debt capital formation, is considered.

Chapters 3 and 4 describe current approaches to small business debt capital formation. Among the types of governmental lending programs explored are micro-lending, direct lending, loan guarantee programs, loan insurance pooling, loan kicker features, and subordinated lending. Chapter 4 concludes with an analysis of the shortcomings of current practice and suggests an innovative system for addressing them for future consideration. Finally, Chapter 5 summarizes the key points made in the book, offers some concluding observations, and looks to the future.

Chapter 1

U.S. SMALL BUSINESSES AND THE GLOBAL ECONOMY

THE IMPORTANCE OF SMALL BUSINESSES TO THE U.S. ECONOMY

Defining "Small Business"

What constitutes a small business varies from place to place. In the United Kingdom, manufacturing firms with 200 or fewer employees are defined to be "small." Japan and Korea consider firms with 300 or fewer employees to be small businesses. Five hundred employees is the upper limit for small businesses in France, Germany, Italy, and the United States (Odaka and Sawai 1999).

The U.S. Small Business Administration (SBA) has further classified small businesses by developing firm size classifications by industry. These classifications are based on either number of employees or sales. Thus, the SBA defines small businesses as follows:

- For most manufacturing and mining businesses—500 or fewer employees;
- For all wholesale trade businesses—100 or fewer employees;
- For most retail and service firms—$5 million in sales;
- For most general and heavy construction firms—$27.5 million in contracts;
- For all special trade contractors—$11.5 million in contracts; and
- For most agricultural businesses—$750,000 in sales.

The Role of Small Business in the U.S. Economy

Small businesses have always played a vital role in the U.S. economy. In Colonial America, farmers, craftsmen, and merchants were at the heart of economic activity. In the Industrial Age, major manufacturing firms had their roots in small-scale, entrepreneurial efforts. Today, in the Information Age, small businesses continue to drive economic growth, particularly in the realm of high technology

The Historical Role

Since the 1970s, when rapid technological change reduced the minimum efficient scale of production, small firms have outperformed large companies in many countries. In the United States, the economic recession of the 1980s and its accompanying widespread unemployment caused a re-evaluation of the significance of small firms to the economy. This elevated stature of small business was further enhanced by the rapid expansion of the service sector. In the decade between 1982 and 1992, the share of total value-added in the construction industry attributable to small firms rose from 78 percent to 88 percent. In manufacturing and mining, the increase was from 23 percent to 25 percent (U.S. Small Business Administration 1996). In general, from 1982 to 1995, there was a 49 percent increase in the number of U.S. small businesses. As of 1994, there were about twenty-two million non-farm businesses, 99 percent of which were classified as small businesses (U.S. Small Business Administration 1996). In 1999, the proportion of total firms in the United States that was defined as being "small" was 99.7 percent (U.S. Census Bureau 2002).

With the results of studies carried out by David Birch in the late 1970s and early 1980s, it became clear that small firms provided the majority of new jobs in the United States. Birch (1981: 8) reported that "whatever else they are doing, large firms are no longer the major providers of new jobs for Americans."

Total employment in the United States grew by approximately one-third between 1976 and 1986. Small businesses accounted for 57 percent of this job growth. During this time period, small firms generated 110 percent of employment in the manufacturing sector. Net employment by small companies increased by 1.3 million workers, while large firms experienced a net loss of 100,000 jobs. Manufacturing firms with less than twenty employees accounted for approximately two-thirds of this growth in employment (U.S. Small Business Administration, 1988). Table 1.1 documents these changes.

Table 1.1
Percentage of Employment Growth by Firm Size and Sector, 1976–86

Firm Size (# of Employees)	All Industries	Manufacturing	Service	Finance
<500	**57.23**	**110.91**	**53.75**	**51.74**
1-19	26.23	64.85	20.76	21.24
20-99	17.43	41.46	15.93	16.15
100-499	13.57	4.60	17.06	14.35
500+	**42.77**	**-10.91**	**46.25**	**48.26**
Total	100.00	100.00	100.00	100.00

Source: U.S. Small Business Administration, Office of Advocacy, Small Business Data Base, USEEM file, version 9 (1987).

An example of this trend comes from the U.S. steel industry. During the period from 1976 to 1986, while the industry, as a whole, lost 48.7 percent of its workers, small steel makers increased their employment by over 48 percent. In terms of share, small firms saw an increase from 4.9 percent to 14.1 percent of all steel-making jobs. Similarly, small firms in other industries where product innovation was occurring at a rapid pace became important sources of employment (U.S. Small Business Administration 1988).

The 1990s saw increasing dominance by small companies in the area of job creation. In the first half of that decade, small businesses generated over three-quarters of the net new jobs. Employment growth in small establishments was 10.5 percent as opposed to 3.7 percent among large companies (U.S. Small Business Administration 1996). During this same time period, businesses with four or fewer employees accounted for the greatest employment growth, at 36.8 percent (U.S. Small Business Administration 1999). Table 1.2 captures the role of small firms in job creation from 1990 to 1998.

Throughout U.S. history, small businesses have played a major role in increased productivity and the development and use of technological innovation (Acs, Tarpley and Phillips 1998). In part, this has been the product

Table 1.2
Net Job Creation by Firm Size, 1990–98 (in Millions)

Firm Size	1990-1995		1997-1998	
	Number	Percent	Number	Percent
< 20 Employees	3.36	49.00	1.39	49.30
< 500 Employees	5.24	76.50	1.73	61.70
Total	6.85	100.00	2.81	100.00

Source: U.S. Census Bureau, *Statistics of U.S. Business,* Cited in Office of Advocacy, U.S. Small Business Administration. http://sba.gov/advo/stats/sbfaq.html, 2002.

of necessity. In order to grow and sustain themselves, they must be nimble and flexible. Unlike large corporations, they cannot afford to sit back and wait to see how things play out. They must lead in their industries or be trampled. Furthermore, small firms, because of their limited resources, have a much smaller margin for error than do larger companies. Everything they do must count if they are to survive. Over the years, this "necessity is the mother of invention" situation has led to numerous major innovative developments by small companies, including but not limited to the airplane, audio tape recorder, heart valve, optical scanner, and the zipper (National Small Business United 2002).

Their very smallness does provide these companies with an advantage. They are capable of reinventing or redirecting themselves very quickly in order to seize rapidly changing market opportunities. By virtue of this, they can gain the competitive advantage of being first to market. This has served not only to generate great wealth for the entrepreneurs who own these firms but has helped the U.S. economy to turn itself around in times of economic recession as well. As an example, a major factor in the turnaround from the recession of the early 1990s was the fact that companies with fewer than five employees generated over one million net jobs in the year between March 1992 and March 1993 (Acs, Tarpley and Phillips 1998).

Small firms have also played a historically significant role as providers of business-to-business services and suppliers of material inputs to large manufacturing companies. In the New England textile industry, for example, over half of all the firms that supplied equipment to the mills employed twenty-five or fewer workers (Howell, McGillivray and Giuffrida 1981).

Another important function played by small businesses in the U.S. economy, over time, has been as a conduit for immigrants into that economy. Thousands of immigrants to the United States have contributed to its economy by using their intelligence, resourcefulness, and sweat equity to build small companies. In turn, the ability to operate enterprises has helped to speed their assimilation process (Acs, Tarpley and Phillips 1998).

The Current Role

Small businesses continue to play a vital role in the current U.S. economy. More than ever before, they are job-creation engines; hotbeds of innovation; havens of opportunity for women, minorities, and the poor; builders of social capital for economic development; and contributors to economic diversity.

Statistics show that the number of people employed by small firms in the U.S. jumped from 55.1 million in 1998 to 68.2 million in 1999 (U.S. Small Business Administration 2001). Small firms create jobs and constitute a significant proportion of total employment in every industrial sector of the economy. At the high end, small firms account for approximately 90 percent of total employment in both the construction and agricultural services industries. Even at the low end, companies with less than 500 employees employ 40 percent of the labor force in the combined industry of transportation, communication, and public utilities. Table 1.3 offers an accounting of small firm employment by industry for 1999.

Employment is not the only area where small businesses make a significant contribution to the U.S. economy. In 1999, they accounted for 47 percent of total sales nationally. They also constituted 50 percent of the nation's gross domestic product (GDP) (U.S. Small Business Administration 2001). Of the industries dominated by small businesses, the fastest growing include computer and data-processing services, counseling and rehabilitation services, credit reporting and collection firms, day care facilities, medical and dental laboratories, outpatient care facilities, physicians' offices, restaurants, and special trade construction contractors (U.S. Department of Labor 2002).

In the current economy, small firms continue to play a leading role in innovation. Recent figures show that small companies generate 55 percent of all new innovations in the United States. On a per-employee basis, they produce twice as many innovations as firms with more than 500 employees. Small companies also receive more patents per sales dollar than do large firms (U.S. Small Business Administration 1999).

Table 1.3
Percent Employment in Firms with Less Than 500 Employees by Industry, 1999

Industry Sector	Employment (in 1000s)	% of Total
Total, Private Sector	68,224.9	58.2
Agricultural Services	2,308.2	90.7
Mining	249.2	45.2
Construction	6,837.6	88.4
Manufacturing	10,390.5	47.9
Trans., Comm. & Public Utilities	3,220.3	40.8
Wholesale Trade	3,544.8	64.9
Retail Trade	12,697.2	51.2
Finance, Insurance, & Real Estate	3,815.9	46.0
Services	25,161.1	66.0

Source: U.S. Small Business Administration, Office of Advocacy. From Data provided by the U.S. Department of Commerce, Bureau of Census, Current Population Survey.

The experience of Silicon Valley in northern California demonstrates the innovative nature and resiliency of small businesses. In the 1970s, about 3,000 electronics firms were in the Valley. Of these, three-quarters had fewer than ten employees. Eighty-five percent employed fewer than 100 people. When Japanese firms took the semiconductor market away from the Silicon Valley, these firms rapidly made the adjustment to producing high value-added electronics goods. This permitted the Valley to remain the economic powerhouse it is today (U.S. Small Business Administration 1999).

The Silicon Valley example suggests another way that small businesses continue to enhance the U.S. economy. Because individual small firms lack the human and financial resources to undertake major research and development efforts, they have created industry networks in some locations. The purposes of these networks are to: (1) pool resources among multiple small companies located in proximity to each other, and/or (2) pool knowledge among regionally proximate firms. This allows these firms to innovate at levels they would otherwise not be able to sustain. In effect, they have cre-ated a region-wide virtual corporation that can have a potentially dramatic positive effect on the region's economy. Put another way, they have built the linkages for the creation of a regional economic system that is capable of sustaining long-term diversity of activity (Saxenian 1991).

When enumerating the contributions of small businesses to the U.S. economy, it is well worth noting the opportunities that these firms have provided to groups who have traditionally lacked economic power— women, minorities, and low-income persons. For women, owning a small business has provided a means for getting out from under the "glass ceil-ing." It has also provided an escape from corporate work practices and expectations that make it difficult to work outside the home and raise a family. In 1997, an estimated eight million women owned their own small businesses (U.S. Small Business Administration 1999). Women are now the predominate group among entrepreneurs.

Individuals from minority groups have also found it difficult to get good jobs and to advance their careers in U.S. corporations. Business ownership has provided them with a viable alternative. In 1997, 3.2 million minority entrepreneurs owned their own businesses (U.S. Small Business Adminis-tration 1999).

With the move to get people off the welfare rolls and into jobs having swept the nation, governments have increasingly looked to small busi-nesses to help achieve this. Small firms hire more employees who were pre-viously on public assistance than do large companies. This should not be surprising given small businesses' dominant performance in job creation in recent decades. The U.S. Small Business Administration (1999) found that, in 1997, small firms employed about 719,000 people receiving public assis-tance, as opposed to large companies, which employed 466,000 such indi-viduals.

THE CHALLENGES POSED BY THE GLOBAL ECONOMY

The global economy poses a variety of challenges to small businesses. Those of major importance include the following:

- Human capital has become more important than physical capital.
- The current economic system is highly diversified and multi-dimensional.
- Business resources are more specialized and there are many choices.
- Global niche markets now exist.

- Innovation can only be fostered by strategic alliances (as noted above).
- Frequent reinvention is necessary for survival.

Some of these challenges were alluded to in the previous discussion, and the ability of small companies to answer them was noted. However, it is worth taking a more detailed look at the challenges as a means of understanding their impact on doing business in today's world, the kinds of companies they engender, and what all of this means for organizations that seek to assist these firms.

Human Capital

There is little doubt that in recent years human capital has outstripped physical and natural capital as the most important form of economic input. Subramanian (1993) has argued that human capital is the most vital form of capital for creating wealth. A recent study by the World Bank found that in breaking down the wealth of countries by types of capital, on average, 64 percent comes from human capital, 20 percent from natural capital and 16 percent from physical capital (Fukuda-Parr 2002).

The shift in the United States from a manufacturing-dominated economy to a service-dominated economy has placed a greater emphasis on managerial skills, technical skills, professional skills of all types, and high-level sales skills. These skill sets typically must be developed through higher education. Even lower-paying jobs in the global economy are requiring higher levels of education and/or more specialized skills (Oliver 2000).

Small businesses, as the leading generators of new jobs, are directly impacted by this new emphasis on human capital. They must be able to find and pay for this human capital if they are to compete effectively. In a recent study, a comparison was drawn between investment in human capital and investment in physical capital in terms of increased productivity. It was found that firms that invested in a 10 percent-higher-than-average education level of their employees achieved 8.6 percent-higher-than-average productivity, while firms that make a 10 percent-higher-than-average investment in physical capital achieve only 3.4 percent-higher-than-average productivity (ElearnFrame 2001). However, small companies have fewer resources than do large corporations to make this essential investment.

A Highly Diversified Economy

The global economy has been described as diverse, dynamic and pluralistic (Saxenian 1991). These characteristics bring challenges to all businesses, but especially to small firms. These latter companies must be aware of a multitude of consumer cultures and how to influence them, they must extend the reach of their marketing efforts, and they must be able to acquire and employ the technology necessary in order to be competitive in this ever-changing economic environment. They must do this with limited resources and, typically, less sophistication than larger businesses have.

Specialized Business Resources

The global economy has brought with it a wide variety of specialized business resources. While this has increased choices, it has also created confusion, especially for small businesses. Entrepreneurs often do not know whom to approach, what to ask for, or how to distinguish among the products and programs available to them.

One example of this is business insurance, where insurance providers are offering new lines of specialized coverage to small companies. These include policies that go well beyond traditional coverage. They also include plans that are tailored to particular professions or industries (Insurance journal.com 2001). It can be overwhelming to small business people to sort out the options and make the right choices.

Capital resource provision has become complex as well. There are a wide variety of debt and equity capital assistance packages. Many entrepreneurs are unsure whether debt or equity financing is appropriate for their company at any given point in its development. Even if they can make this distinction, they are often confused by the array of products within each.

Global Niche Markets

Large global corporations, with extensive financial resources, have captured the general markets. This has made it virtually impossible for small companies to compete for these markets. It has forced small firms to try to find little niches in these larger markets where consumer demand is not being met. That is, new small entrants into global markets must focus ever more minutely on groups of consumers who are under-served or whose demands are not being met by competitors (Mendoza 2001).

Mendoza (2001) tells the story of RedWagons.com, which sells Red Flyer toy wagons via the Internet. RedWagons.com could not compete with the big Internet toy companies, like Amazon.com; so, they took advantage of the fact that Amazon and others sold only 3 or 4 lines of Red Flyer wagons by offering the entire line. This opened a niche market consisting of collectors and other people who wanted access to the entire line and could get it nowhere else.

Such global niche markets can be quite lucrative. Berger (2000) reports that the fire-and-safety-products niche market employs about two million people and is worth almost $40 billion per year. Finding these markets is the trick, and being able to manage the risk that the market one finds is accessible and adequate to sustain the business is the challenge.

Strategic Alliances

Small businesses are at the forefront of innovation, if for no other reason than that they have to be in order to survive and thrive in the global economy. They are important users of new technologies and outstrip large companies in their innovation efficiency (Oliver 2000). Several statistics from National Small Business United (2002) bear this out:

- Small firms are more than four times as likely to use federal dollars for basic research than are large companies;
- The percentage of employees of small businesses who are research scientists or engineers is about 6.5 percent, as opposed to approximately 4 percent in large firms;
- Small businesses receive 11 percent of their R&D budgets from the federal government, while 26 percent of the R&D budgets of large firms comes from the federal government;
- Small companies with intellectual property average 61 employees, with 19 percent of these in R&D; large firms with intellectual property average 12,879 employees, with 3 percent of these in R&D.

Because small companies do not have the R&D resources, including manpower, that large firms have, the former must build alliances with other entities to achieve their goals. The focus of these networks is information/knowledge exchange. Partners typically include other businesses in the same industry but not necessarily direct competitors, colleges and universities, customers, and research laboratories and institutions, among others (White, et al. 1988). There are a number of examples of larger companies, like Apple Computers, that have invested in small firms in their geographic area that make products complementary to their own (Saxenian 1991). By engaging in these latter relationships with larger companies, the small firms are able to get the equity capital they need to develop their products and expand their markets.

Frequent Reinvention

An important part of the global economy is rapid change. Small businesses that cannot reinvent themselves in order to adapt to this change are vulnerable to failure. On the one hand, this represents a substantial challenge to small firms because they may lack the resources to make dramatic shifts in direction. On the other hand, small firms are more likely to be nimble enough to make such changes more quickly and smoothly than their larger competitors.

Changes may come in any of the key areas of business: competition, customers, market, and the company, itself (Partners for Small Business Excellence 2000). From wherever it comes, the business must be prepared to move quickly so as to minimize financial damage. An example of this is the case of a small grocery store in California that had a large chain grocery store open its doors a few yards away. Only a major reinvention could save the small store. The solution was to change their product line and become a sports catalog store (Partners for Small Business Excellence 2000).

All of these challenges have created a situation wherein the ability to adjust to constantly changing circumstances is essential. In many ways, this is the ideal environment for entrepreneurship because innovation is paramount. Yet, we cannot merely assume that anyone with a propensity to be entrepreneurial will succeed in this new business environment. The new global entrepreneur must be highly skilled in various aspects of starting, operating, and growing a business. More than ever before, entrepreneurs are made and not born (Shefsky 1994; Lichtenstein and Lyons 2001). In light of this, what is required is a transformation of our entrepreneurs and of entrepreneurship in the United States: a qualitative change in how we think about entrepreneurship and how we go about supporting it (Lichtenstein and Lyons 2001).

IMPLICATIONS FOR ENTERPRISE DEVELOPMENT ASSISTANCE

Given the continued importance of small businesses to the vitality and growth of the U.S. economy, the authors argue that there is ample reason to involve government in assisting these companies to achieve success as a legitimate part of local and regional economic development efforts. The real question is how best to do that, given the challenges these firms face.

Because successful entrepreneurship hinges upon the acquisition and mastery of a skill set, success in assisting entrepreneurs must reside in facilitating this process. The skills required are various. They include the skills necessary to create the product or service to be sold; the skills involved in conducting the day-to-day operations of an enterprise; the ability to recognize and seize viable opportunities and create innovative solutions to problems; and the self-awareness, accountability, emotional, and capability skills that constitute personal maturity (Lichtenstein and Lyons 2001; Lichtenstein and Lyons 1996). These skills are not built through arms-length, transactional relationships. Their acquisition and mastery are achieved through transformational processes involving peers, mentors, partners, and a host of others (Lichtenstein and Lyons 2001). If enterprise development assistance is to help transform the entrepreneur, the entrepreneur's company and, ultimately, the community or region in the global economy, it must coordinate and foster these transformational relationships.

The next chapter continues to build an understanding of debt capital formation and its relationship to the transformational process.

REFERENCES

Acs, Z. J., F. A. Tarpley, and B. D. Phillips. 1998. *The New American Evolution.* Washington, D.C.: U.S. Small Business Administration, Office of Advocacy.

Berger, S. 2000. "Traditional Industries Venture into E-Commerce." *Jerusalem Post,* 12. Internet Edition, October 18. (http://www.jpost.com/Editions/2000/10/18 /Business/Business.13906.html).

Birch, D. 1981. "Who Creates Jobs?" *The Public Interest,* 65 (Fall).

ElearnFrame. 2001. "Continued Effort to Reduce Costs and Improve ROI." (http://www.learnframe.com/aboutlearning/page24.asp).

Fukuda-Parr, S. 2002. "The Americas Business Forum: Forum Speeches-COMMITTEE IV: Human Development and Corporate Responsibility." (http://www.sice.oas.org/FTAA/cartage/keynot/comite4.asp).

Howell, J. M, B. E. McGillivray, and A. J. Giuffrida. 1981. *History of Small Business in New England.* Economic Research on Small Business: The Environment for Entrepreneurship and Small Business, Summary Analysis of the Regional Research Reports. Washington, D.C.: U.S. Small Business Administration (June).

InsuranceJournal.com. 2001. "Kemper Targets Small Business Market with Specialized Coverages." (http://www.insurancejournal.com/html/ijweb/breaking news/archives/national/na1100/na1115003.htm). November 15.

Lichtenstein, G. A., and T. S. Lyons. 1996. *Incubating New Enterprises: A Guide to Successful Practice.* Washington, D.C.: The Aspen Institute.

Lichtenstein, G. A., and T. S. Lyons. 2001. "The Entrepreneurial Development System: Transforming Business Talent and Community Economies." *Economic Development Quarterly* 15, 1:3–20.

Mendoza, M. 2001. "Focus on Your Niche." (http://www.powerhomebiz.com/vol62/niche.htm).

National Small Business United. 2002. "Brief Statistics Showing that Small Business Drives America's Economic Engine." (http://www.nsbu.org/statistics2.htm).

Odaka, K. and M. Sawai. 1999. *Small Firms, Large Concerns: The Development of Small Business in Comparative Perspective.* Oxford, UK: Oxford University Press.

Oliver, R. W. 2000. "The Future of Small Businesses: Trends for a New Century." (http://www.sbtrends2000.com).

Partners for Small Business Excellence. 2000. "Reinvention: Today's Business Imperative." *Small Business Success Magazine.* (http://www.smallbizpartners.com /success/XIIarticles/reinvent.html).

Saxenian, A. 1991. "The Origins and Dynamics of Production Networks in Silicon Valley." *Research Policy* 20: 423–437.

Shefsky, L. E. 1994. *Entrepreneurs Are Made not Born.* New York: McGraw-Hill.

Subramanian, R. 1993. "Human Capitalism: The Japanese Enterprise System as World Model." *Journal of Small Business Management,* April.

U.S. Census Bureau. 2002. *Statistics of U.S. Businesses, Tabulations by Enterprise Size.* (http://www.census.gov/csd/susb/usst99.xls).

U.S. Department of Labor. 2002. *Advocacy Research,* cited in U.S. Small Business Administration, Office of Advocacy (http://bus.colorado.edu/faculty/meyer/ sba.htm).

U.S. Small Business Administration. 1988. *Small Business in the American Economy.* Washington, D.C.: Office of Advocacy.

U.S. Small Business Administration. 1996. *The Facts About Small Business,* November.

U.S. Small Business Administration. 1987. Office of Advocacy, Small Business Data Base, USEEM file, version 9.

U.S. Small Business Administration. 1999. *The State of Small Business: A Report to the President, 1998.* Washington, D.C.: U.S. Government Printing Office.

U.S. Small Business Administration. 2001. *Small Business Economic Indicators for 1999.* Washington D.C.: Office of Advocacy.

White, M., J. Braczyk, A. Ghobadian, and J. Nieburh. 1988. "Small Firms' Innovation: Why Regions Differ." London: Policy Studies Institute.

Chapter 2

THE IMPORTANCE OF DEBT CAPITAL TO SMALL BUSINESS

Obtaining investment capital is one issue faced by the small and/or fledgling company. It is only one of many, and may not be the most important challenge in many situations. Or, it may become the critical issue only after other preconditions are met, such as the adequate skill and emotional readiness of the business's principal entrepreneurs. Yet, capital is important to small business success and is particularly challenging for reasons that will be described.

The purpose of this chapter is to provide the context for understanding the importance of small-business, debt capital formation. The chapter has four parts that lead from the general setting to specific issues. The first section provides a general understanding of capital formation and its importance to small business. It starts with a discussion of the financial intermediary system. The section relates the need for small business financing and then describes the difficulty current systems have in making that kind of capital available. The second section investigates the role of capital formation for business incubation. The third section focuses on debt capital as one aspect of capital formation, and the fourth section states the need for governmental involvement in capital formation and what form it should take. This chapter prepares the reader for the discussions of specific governmental interventions presented in Chapters 3 and 4.

THE ROLE OF CAPITAL FORMATION IN SMALL BUSINESS SUCCESS

Financial Intermediary System

The first step in the process of economic development for any society is to produce a surplus. Then, some of that surplus must be saved, that is, not consumed. An individual can save and store savings in a variety of forms, including monetary forms or as a stash of storable commodities, but saving is not money. Saving is the human time and skill necessary to produce the equivalent stored surplus.

Human time and talent is perishable. Each day that it is not employed is lost. Economic development requires that society translate some savings into investment to create more efficient production methods and generate more surplus in the future. The product of investment can take many forms, including new tools, processes, knowledge, education, or training.

The translation of savings into investment requires intermediary organizations. These intermediaries act as go-betweens or brokers. They link the saver, the one with a surplus, with the appropriate investor, someone wanting to rent the surplus to free up time to create new technologies (Hamlin and Lyons 1996).

For a society to build a sophisticated economy, it must have an array of strong intermediary organizations. A society must possess various investment vehicles to match different saving and investment needs. An economy is more successful if it has a rich variety of intermediaries that, in turn, generate a highly diverse array of investments and business activities. Some intermediaries must serve high-risk endeavors while others rent surplus to lower-risk activities. Some investment vehicles provide equity capital while others offer debt capital. Some must be available for the long term while others need only assume risk for a short time (Hamlin and Lyons 1996).

The financial intermediary system should translate savings into investment in varying magnitudes, ranging from billions of dollars to promote heavy industrial and advanced technological development, to a few hundred dollars for micro-enterprise creation. Investment vehicles should be available for both collateralized transactions and unsecured transactions. The intermediary system should be capable of channeling society's surplus into human investment, such as education and training, as well as into capital assets such as buildings, machinery, and equipment. The system must be able to focus savings on both public infrastructure and private assets. Gaps in the array of intermediaries produce holes in the economy that take the form of underdeveloped industries, unmet consumer needs, lagging communities, weak business incubation, and public sector fiscal stress (Hamlin and Lyons 1996).

Neglect of the Middle of the Risk/Reward Spectrum

Critical to the intermediary process is matching the risks that savers and investors are willing to take with the potential rewards associated with an investment. For reasons not totally understood, the middle range of the risk/reward spectrum is often not well served. On the one hand, most savers are risk averse, preferring to put their wealth into very conservative organizations such as banks. In order to protect those deposits, banks act out their conservative role.

In sophisticated and aggressive investment environments, venture capitalists spring up, often with governmental incentives, to provide another kind of financial intermediary. Venture capitalists focus on the very high-risk sector, generally technology-intensive businesses that hold out the promise of a several-hundred-percent return on investment.

The middle of the risk/reward spectrum includes the range between conventional bank financing and venture capital. Private institutions are poorly developed to deal with the medium-risk client. Government does a poor job of sharing risk. It does not institutionalize medium-risk, risk-sharing mechanisms the way it does for conventional banking. Institutions similar to the FDIC and the FSLIC are generally not available in the middle realm (Hamlin and Duma 1999).

Stock and corporate bond markets are forms of financial intermediaries with higher risk than bank deposits. U.S. society has moved toward them as a form of savings. Insurance companies and pension funds (including 401Ks) have recently broadened their approaches to investing to include this somewhat higher-risk investment. Yet, stock and bond markets generally serve the investment needs of higher capitalization businesses, not small businesses (Hamlin 1998).

Unresponsiveness of Conventional Intermediaries to Small Business Needs

Several activities critical to the vitality of an advanced economy take place in the middle of the risk/reward spectrum. As is fully delineated in Chapter 1, key to the development of a strong and broad economy is small business development. By virtue of its own diversity, the small business sector of the economy helps to diversify the greater national economy. Small businesses represent a rich and varied network of suppliers, sub-contractors, and distributors that work in a complementary fashion with large corporations, augmenting the efficiency, flexibility, and balance of the overall economy (Solomon 1986). They perfect markets by adding to the number of buyers and sellers of products and raw materials. In accordance with the ecological principle known as Ashby's Law, the increased economic diversity afforded by small businesses yields stability in the economic system (Baldwin 1985).

Despite the importance of small business, banks historically have not been sufficiently responsive to small business capital needs. When banks lend to small businesses, loans tend to be short term (three to five years) and high interest (several percent over prime). As collateral-oriented lenders, banks must often be more concerned about securing adequate collateral coverage to prepare for when the business fails, rather than investing in a business's future success. While this orientation may be justified by bankers' mandate to protect depositors' interests, relying on conventional banking for a high percentage of small business capital leaves small businesses poorly served during several phases of their life cycle (Hamlin 1998). If businesses are under capitalized at these critical points they often fail. These important periods include: (1) start-up, (2) rapid growth, (3) new product development, and (4) economic downturns (Berger and Udel 1998).

The start-up phase will be described in the following section on incubation. Here we will talk about (2), (3) and (4).

Rapid Growth

If a small business is successful, it might experience a stage of very rapid growth. This is often the period of greatest financial need. In many markets a stage is reached where gradual growth is not possible. Larger scale facilities and equipment might become necessary for the next stage of expansion. Sometimes this quantum leap in business activity is necessary for survival. Either you grow rapidly or fall behind. The originator of a new product or service, for example, must move to capture significant market share before competition moves into the field (Berger and Udel 1998).

Not only do all inputs to the production process increase at this crucial juncture, but also receivables grow rapidly, as the business must "finance" a larger number of customers. Receivables also "age" more during this period, as the customer base becomes larger, more diverse, and perhaps more geographically dispersed. It may also be the time to change, add or expand locations, and increase distribution channels. At some point in the rapid growth phase, a total reorganization of the business operation is often necessary, with associated costs.

Capital needs during the period of accelerated growth tend to outstrip both personal and business collateral. This shortage in coverage will likely put the collateral-oriented lending of conventional banking out of reach. Without an alternative, growth will be stifled or worse.

New Product Line

A key to small business success is the ability to continually identify new directions or products that spin-off of the existing product line. Continual reinvention of a business and its product lines is necessary for survival in a global environment. Initially, small business managers are smart to focus on a particular niche market, but in the long run this makes them vulnerable to changes in society's tastes and preferences. Small businesses might be more adroit at making needed shifts than are larger corporations, as described in the previous chapter, but only if they have the capital to act.

Developing new product lines requires expenditures on new equipment, new distribution systems, employee training and recruitment, and new marketing strategies. Lack of middle-risk capital reduces small businesses' ability to add new products and services and make needed adjustments.

Business Cycles

Small businesses are particularly vulnerable to national economic cycles. Not only might the demand for their primary product or service be susceptible to national economic swings, but their community or market area might also be particularly hard hit. Imagine a building materials retailer who suffers the start-up costs of new space and inventory and then, in the business's third year, the nation slides into a recession. He/she still suffers large debt service payments from those start-up expenditures. Some of the start-up loans may begin to balloon.

Simultaneously, the business suffers declining or stagnant sales as building construction activity declines. Building construction is generally the first to turn down in a recession. Moreover, if this retailer operates in a community with a high percentage of employment in consumer durable goods manufacturing (e.g. refrigerators), then the entire market area of the building materials supplier would be hit by the second stage of the downturn, when consumer durable sales decline.

The above example is hypothetical, but new small businesses generally take about five years to get on their feet. Since national economic cycles have historically come every five years or less, nearly all start-up businesses must survive at least one recession before they are continuously profitable. Receiving some interim financing, or an extension on existing debt, could be critical to that survival (Hamlin 2002)

Difficult Collateral

In addition to issues related to business life cycles and national economic cycles, some businesses are not well served by collateral-oriented lenders in any environment. Their assets are not easily valued as collateral. As an example, companies with paper assets such as insurance agencies find it difficult to qualify for bank loans. Likewise businesses with heavy receivable burdens, such as temporary worker agencies, badly need a bridge loan but are considered to have soft receivables. They must often pay the full salary of the "temp," and then wait two or three months before their clients make payments to them. Similarly, manufacturers with specialized and illiquid equipment find that banks do not value the potential for equipment resale highly. A winery has a high percentage of its net worth tied up in "work in progress" that banks have trouble valuing. These kinds of businesses and many others are not well served in an environment without any mechanism for medium-risk financing (Hamlin 1999).

If the need is great, why doesn't middle risk/reward financing come into existence on its own in response to market demand? Certainly, higher-risk customers would have to pay more or give up more to the risk-taking investor in order to receive capital, but this scenario is well understood in the venture capital process. To a minor extent middle-risk financing has grown up naturally. Seed capitalists have developed an array of innovative but ad hoc mechanisms for extracting greater benefit from a deal to compensate for the greater risk. These methods include higher interest rates, equity kickers, and royalty arrangements. Yet, no broad-based and sophisticated intermediary system has ever come into existence without government playing at least two important roles. These roles are: (1) legitimizing and sanctioning an institutional structure and process, and (2) sharing some of the risk. The government's role in facilitating small business capital is central to this book.

THE RELATIONSHIP BETWEEN CAPITAL FORMATION AND SMALL BUSINESS INCUBATION

Incubation is the process a start-up business goes through during its first three to five years of existence. The word "incubation" often refers to assistance given to businesses to help them through this period. During this time the business faces many challenges, the response to which could determine the business's survival or future course. Some of these challenges result from the inexperience of the business's leaders while others come from the unique situation the start-up business experiences. The business's challenges include new product development, logistics, marketing, distribution, and finance. Challenges also include the skill level, psychology, and commitment of the principals of the firm.

Obtaining investment capital is one issue faced by the fledgling company. It is only one of many, and may not be the most important challenge in many situations. Or, it may become critical only after other preconditions are resolved. However, the start-up phase for any business is financially difficult. New businesses experience heavy financial burdens from the need to purchase new machinery and equipment, set up marketing and distribution systems, train employees, buy initial inventory and overcome the cash flow problems associated with customer receivables.

Some claim that undercapitalization is the most common cause of new business failures. Often, new businesses are unprofitable for three to five years from start-up. If they run low on funds during this time they might be forced to make decisions that hurt the long-term viability of the business. It is common for businesses short on capital to focus on inventory and production to meet current demand and to be too thrifty on critical components of future success, such as marketing and distributions system development.

Bankers are reluctant to lend conventionally during these early years, for the reasons discussed in previous sections. They know the risks. The caution caused by an entrepreneur's unknown track record is compounded if banks see weak or distorted income and balance sheet statements. They know the signs. Once the downward slide begins, few are interested in helping out. A start-up business should have more than enough capital to sustain itself through the incubation period, it is argued.

On the other hand, the most important variable for small business success might be the knowledge and skill level of the entrepreneur. Financing is critical and underfunding could be a fatally inhibiting factor at a key period of business growth. However, too much financing too early is also problematic. Being undercapitalized is a common problem for small business, but entrepreneurs need to fully understand how to use financing. Too much funding too soon, before the firm and its principals are prepared for rapid growth can lead fledgling business leaders astray. With plenty of initial cash they become less focused on the bottom line. They might put too much money in the wrong facets of the business. In short, in the beginning stages of a business, modest funding sometimes focuses the mind.

If the financing takes the form of loans, too much early debt also hurts the balance sheet, the income statement, and cash flow, particularly during early periods of modest sales. This situation is exacerbated if excessive debt causes the interest rate the business is charged to augment because of a weaker balance sheet. (These issues are discussed in the next section.) Excessive government-sponsored debt acquired early in the business's life can reduce the ability of the business to find private financing. If the balance sheet already has a high debt-to-equity ratio, private lenders will not lend more until the ratio is brought down.

DEBT CAPITAL AS AN ASPECT OF CAPITAL FORMATION

Two kinds of capital a business can raise are debt capital and equity. Finding the right balance between them is important. A common view of these two is that equity is what owners have, and debt is a loan from someone else. This is too simplistic. A better approach is to look at how each functions, and what impact each has on the business, the entrepreneur and the capitalists. One should also understand that equity vs. debt is not an absolute dichotomy. A continuum of mixed financial intermediary instruments is possible.

In a few ways, debt and equity capital are similar.

- Both debt and equity capital are forms of funding that an entrepreneur can use to build a business.
- In both cases, the suppliers of capital, the investors, are looking for an adequate return on investment in relationship to the amount of risk involved.
- In both cases, the investor will exercise some control over the business and the entrepreneur in order to minimize risk, although the form of control will be different.

Some differences between the two forms of capital are:

- the levels of risk experienced by each stakeholder,
- the rate and nature of the return on investment,
- the placement of each on the balance sheet,
- the effect of each on the income statement,
- the impact of each on cash flow,
- the tax treatment of the return on investment faced by the investor,
- the tax impact on the borrowing business,
- the amount and nature of control over the business exercised by the investor, and
- the longevity of the relationship between business and investor.

Each will be described below.

Risk

With respect to risk, the difference between equity investments and debt is really more of a continuum than an absolute dichotomy. At one end of the spectrum, equity investors buy common stock in a company or are partners or sole proprietors. They are owners, and their return-on-investment is directly related to the success of the business. At the other extreme, investors are lenders, loan providers who are promised a fixed rate of return no matter what the success of the business. If the business completely fails, of course, that promise might not be kept. Between these two extremes are a variety of mixed forms including preferred stock, bonds, convertible paper, and loans with equity features, to name a few.

Equity investment is the most risky for the provider of funds. Receiving some capital injection in the form of equity reduces risk for the business since the equity capital usually does not have to be given back. In the event of dissolution, the senior securities, primarily loans and bonds, are covered first. Intermediate securities such as preferred stock are covered next. Equity investors recover their investment only if any value is left after more senior commitments are honored. Being the most risky, equity injections are therefore the most difficult capital to raise.

Form of Pay Out: Dividends v. Interest

Equity investors receive dividends or other profit distributions. Lenders earn interest. Interest payments are often higher than dividends as a percent of the original investment even though equity investment is more risky. This is because, in addition to profit distributions, equity holders hope for a capital gain, an increase in the value of the original investment.

The dichotomy between the forms of return on equity and return on debt is also somewhat false. A variety of other forms is possible. Preferred stock dividends, as an example, can behave more like interest than dividends. Interest payments are periodic promised payment. Common stock dividends only occur if surpluses are available to be distributed. Preferred stock dividends are an example of a hybrid. Preferred dividends are promised, fixed payment. The promise can be broken without legal consequences, but the promised preferred dividend must be paid before common stock dividends are allowed.

Balance Sheet Issues

On the balance sheet an equity investment is listed as paid-in capital. While this is an offset to assets, it is not considered a liability to the business since it need not be paid back. A loan to the business is also a charge against assets but is listed under debt as a liability, an obligation to be paid back. As has been shown, debt and equity injections can look and behave similarly even though one is considered to be a strong point on the balance sheet and the other is considered a burden. This distinction is so strong that someone analyzing a balance sheet uses ratios such as "liabilities as a percentage of net worth," or debt-to-equity ratio. The "current ratio" is the ratio of current assets such as receivables to current liabilities (payment on debt during the next periodic cycle).

A business that incurs too much debt will have weak ratios, and investors will look upon it unfavorably for future capital injections, including bank loans. As alluded to in the previous section, the timing of debt capital infusions is crucial. If a new business takes on too much debt too early, and does not use the funds to maximum benefit, the business will be saddled with a weak balance sheet. It may find that new loans are more difficult to obtain.

Some tricks are occasionally used. Assume the business offers an investor, such as a local revolving fund, preferred stock, with an agreement to buy the stock back over ten years. The business commits to make a periodic dividend payment to the investor and a periodic repayment of principal just as if it were a loan. Yet, the revolving fund investment shows up on the balance sheet as equity not debt, theoretically strengthening the balance sheet rather than weakening it. In this way the revolving fund enhances the business's chances of private financing rather than diminishing it. (See local revolving fund, Chapter 3.)

Income Statement Issues

Debt and equity also effect the income statement of the business differently. The price of a loan is interest. Interest is considered a cost of doing business. It is listed as an expense and reduces profits. This makes the business income statement look weaker. The payment for equity investments takes the form of a dividend or similar distribution. Dividends are not an expense and do to reduce income as shown on the income statement. They are a distribution of profits after income and expenses have been calculated. Too much debt early in the life of a business could increase interest costs, making a positive bottom line on the income statement more difficult.

Impact on Cash Flow

Cash flow and income are often very different flows. Some expenses, such as depreciation, are non-cash expenditures that reduce income but not cash flow. Also, acquiring new investment capital represents positive cash flow in the short run, without sales revenues. In the intermediate term a high debt load will strain cash flow. Debt service, including both interest and principal payments, will be a drain on cash flow for the life of the loan. Businesses that receive too much in loans early in their life and do not spend the funds optimally will face an elongated period of perpetual cash-flow concerns. Inexperienced business owners are often anxious to obtain financing, but do not fully appreciate the cash-flow effects down the road.

Investor Tax Treatment

From the perspective of the provider of investment capital, dividends and interest are treated differently. Interest earned must be added to the investor's own taxable income. The same is true for dividends received, except that many for-profit, C corporations are allowed some dividend exemption. If the equity investment is in the form of a partnership arrangement, profits pass, for tax purposes, to the partners who then add their share of the profits to their own tax calculations. This provides two advantages. First it avoids the double taxation of dividends, the situation where a corporation pays taxes, distributes profits as dividends and then the investor must pay taxes again on dividend income. Second, non-cash expenses like depreciation can be deducted before taxable profits are determined. If, after depreciation expenses, profits are negative, the partnership can pass the negative profit to the partner who can, in many cases, use the paper loss to reduce his/her own taxable income. A partnership agreement can legally distribute the benefits of the investment unequally. The partner most in need receives cash and the partner most able to benefit from them receives paper losses, for example.

Business Tax Impact

For the business making payments to investors, interest payments on a loan or a bond are a cost of doing business. Interest is deducted from profits before calculating taxes, creating a tax advantage for the business. Dividends are not an expense of doing business but are considered to be a distribution of profits. Dividends are not deductible to the business but are taxable to the investor, creating the infamous "double taxation of dividends." If the business is not overly burdened with debt service, causing the cash flow issues discussed early in this chapter, debt capital provides its own kind of tax advantage. However, this advantage is most pronounced for businesses in the highest corporate income tax bracket. Small, fledgling businesses are less likely to be in that bracket and less likely to benefit from interest expenses.

Control

The most obvious difference between debt and equity capital is that the equity investor holds some form of ownership in the business and therefore some amount of control. This is not a simple issue and control relationships can vary widely. Control may depend on whether the company has multiple classes of stock, preferred stock, or limited partnership arrangements, to name a few examples. Generally, taking on equity investors will mean that the principals of the business must give up some control, thus the need to keep debt and equity in balance.

Lenders also want to exercise some control. In some cases this control is non-legal, informal control, but forceful. Many banks, for example, engage in a practice called "relationship lending." They strongly suggest that, if the small business wants future bank cooperation, the small business should do all of its banking with that bank. This strategy is both to generate banking business and to keep informal control over the small business's debt load (Berger and Udel 1995).

Longevity of the Relationship

Related to the issue of control is the question of longevity of the relationship. When a business takes out a loan, its owners know that the debt capitalist will be out of the picture once the loan is successfully paid in full. This is seldom so certain with any kind of equity investment, although stock buy-back agreements can make an equity investment look like a loan in this regard.

Role of Debt

To summarize the discussions presented in this section, debt capital has an important role to play in small business incubation and long-term success. It offers some tax advantages, offers the business greater certainty of relationships and facilitates maintenance of control over the business. Debt capital is often easier to obtain than equity.

Small businesses and business service providers should realize that forms of capital bridge the gambit between pure debt and pure equity. A wide variety of combinations and hybrids are legally possible. They should also realize that a balance in types of business funding should be maintained, and that the mix should be based on the advantages of each form to a business's unique situation. Businesses should be cognizant of the effect of their capital-raising efforts on their tax situation, their control of the business, their relationship with capitalists over time and capacity to raise various types of capital in the future.

Most importantly, the timing of capital raising is critical. Entrepreneurs should not take the attitude that they should pursue any kind of funds they can get their hands on. Use of capital should be planned carefully, which implies that entrepreneurs have the knowledge, skill, and emotional capacity to use the funds wisely.

GOVERNMENTAL INVOLVEMENT IN SMALL BUSINESS DEBT-CAPITAL FORMATION

Rationale for Governmental Intervention

In a market-driven system, one must provide justification for governmental involvement in economic activity. Generally we assume that if a free market is able to supply a needed good or service, we leave it to the free competitive market to do so. The phrase "free competitive market" is not the same as a laissez-faire system. Rather, it implies a marketplace that meets certain criteria. If the market does not meet those criteria, then it is not a good allocator of goods, services, and resources. Economists have defined a free competitive market as one that realizes "perfect competition." In its ideal state such a market has the following characteristics (Lyons and Hamlin 2001):

1. a large number of buyers and sellers participate in the marketplace such that no one has a significant impact on the market;
2. the product sold in the market is highly divisible; it can be purchased in small individual units;
3. each unit of product is indistinguishable in quantity and quality;
4. an auction market procedure establishes the price of each unit based on supply and demand;
5. all buyers and sellers possess perfect knowledge about functioning of the market, including price and quality;
6. no externalized costs or benefits result from behavior of the market participants (Mahanty, 1980).

A model or paradigm expresses an ideal condition that might never fully exist. A sound market that properly allocates goods and services is one that approaches the model of perfect competition. If a market has serious flaws in comparison to the model, it might not allocate goods, services and resources efficiently. It may experience market failure. Such a situation causes distortions and instabilities throughout the economy (Lyons and Hamlin 2001).

Clearly the provision of some goods and services does not come close to matching the model of perfect competition. One strategy in this case is for government to act to perfect the markets. In other words, if market imperfections cause dislocations that induce businesses to behave contrary to public policy, discover how the characteristics of that market deviate from the model of perfect competition. Government should act to bring the behavior of the market closer to the model (Lyons and Hamlin 2001). To restate this idea, if private markets do not operate efficiently, or do not produce outcomes desired by public policy, then the public sector should carefully use both carrot and stick to nudge the private sector in the proper direction. The stick represents laws and regulations that enforce minimum standards of behavior; the carrot represents incentives for more optimal behavior. These incentives take the form of regulatory relaxation, financial inducements, coordination, or information, to name a few (Lyons and Hamlin 2001).

Governmental Involvement in the Intermediary System

The intermediary system might be the most important and the most fragile aspect of the economic development process. Inducing the saver to rent his/her surplus wealth to an investor requires a high level of knowledge and trust at both ends, and good communication throughout the system. All of these factors can breakdown easily and quickly if not well managed. Trust is a state of mind that can be destroyed by one major event. To be able to trust the system, the enormous risk associated with the intermediary process must be mitigated through risk sharing. Required knowledge includes a rational understanding of the risk involved and good communication includes quick information about price, quantity, and news that could affect future trends in both the security involved and the world economy.

Public sector involvement in the intermediary system represents the essence of intersectoral synergy, balancing the public interest with a need to reward savings and risk. Careful public intervention is a method of market perfection since numerous imperfections make capital markets shaky without basic public involvement. Government must institutionalize the intermediary process and share some of the risk. Without a partnership with public involvement, an adequate intermediary system would not exist. Examples of existing governmental involvement include regulation of securities markets, establishment and regulation of the banking industry, provision of deposit insurance, and the willingness to back deposit insurance with government funds. In recent decades government has become more involved in the regulation of derivatives, restriction of erratic securities price movements, and attempts to ensure honesty in communications.

Those societies that have not developed good intermediaries find economic growth difficult. Intermediaries would not occur to the degree or in the variety necessary for the full array of economic activity to flourish without governmental involvement. Even in highly advanced industrialized societies the variety of intermediaries is often inadequate. In one culture, large corporations have no trouble raising capital, while small business development stagnates. In another country, both low-risk capital and venture capital may be abundant, but intermediate-risk, seed capital remains non-existent (Hamlin 1998; Hamlin and Lyons 1996).

As described at the beginning of this chapter, society must possess various investment vehicles to match different saving and investment needs. An economy is more successful if it has a rich variety of intermediaries that, in turn, generate a highly diverse array of investments and business activities. This variety includes a spectrum of risk/reward situations, both debt and equity capital, a continuum of time horizons, varying sizes or amounts, and a variety of purposes. Geography is also a variable. Some parts of the country, and some urban neighborhoods, are considered a higher risk and are less likely to receive investment capital without higher reward (Hamlin 1998; Hamlin and Lyons 1996).

Any discontinuities in this array of intermediary arrangements will produce holes in the economy. These holes take the form of industrial sectors that are not fully developed, consumer needs that are poorly met, gaps in the life cycle of businesses that short-circuit business growth, weak responses to the challenges of globalization, declining communities, and lagging public sector revenues (Hamlin and Lyons 1996).

Some ways in which government acts as a partner with the intermediary systems are: (1) to maintain a stable monetary system so as to monetize the intermediary process; (2) to regulate financial intermediaries; (3) to create a central financial intermediary which acts as the banker's banker; (4) to share risk by insuring deposits; (5) to legally sanction an array of intermediary organizations to serve the variety of intermediary needs described above; (6) to carry a greater share of the risk in communities that are, themselves, at-risk, and (7) to invest selectively its own surplus in private sector activities (Hamlin and Lyons 1996).

With respect to (5) above, some intermediaries are common and seem obvious. They include banks, stock markets, bond markets, and pension funds. Alone, these traditional vehicles leave huge gaps in the continuum of investment needs. Venture capital, seed capital, and pre-venture capital organizations must also be present to provide for high-risk/high-growth investments. Loan guarantees, insurance pools and secondary market support must allow for medium-risk loans not provided by traditional banks. This is discussed in the next section. Also, organizations that target declining communities to channel investment capital into them must be present to overcome the downward spiral of market failure leading to community decline. Government's role in all cases is not to become a primary source of capital, but to perfect markets and become a catalyst for increased private savings and investment across the spectrum of investment needs (Hamlin and Lyons 1996).

Attempts to Provide Middle-Risk Financing

Because of the importance of small business growth for national and local economic development, government must intervene to ensure the presence of midrisk intermediaries that serve small businesses. Governments at all levels have attempted various means to improve the intermediary process in the mid-range of the risk/reward spectrum. They have attempted to channel capital to promising small businesses not eligible for or fully served by conventional bank lending. They also sometimes target their efforts at particular communities perceived as higher risk and therefore have greater difficulties raising investment capital. The purpose of these programs should be to perfect intermediary markets so as to channel funds to small businesses at appropriate times and amounts. Government should try to institutionalize a system of midrisk financing and share some of the risk, where appropriate, for the business and society.

Methods for providing midrisk debt capital include direct government loans, revolving loan funds, subordinated loans, loan guarantees, industrial development revenue bonds, loan insurance, bond insurance, secondary money markets, and loans with equity or royalty features, to name a few. The next two chapters will describe in detail six of these concepts. It will offer examples of as well as critique specific governmental programs that use them.

REFERENCES

Baldwin, J. H. 1985. *Environmental Planning and Management.* Boulder, CO: Westview Press.

Berger, A. N., and G. F. Udel. 1995. "Relationship Lending and Lines of Credit in Small Firm Finance." *Journal of Business* 68: 351–382.

Berger, A .N., and G. F. Udel. 1998. "The Economics of Small Business Finance: The Roles of Private Equity and Debt Markets in the Financial Growth Cycle." *Journal of Banking and Finance* 22: 613–673.

Hamlin, R. E. 1998. *The Capital Access Program: An Evaluation of Economic Benefit.* Lansing, MI: The Michigan Jobs Commission.

Hamlin, R. E. 1999. Capital Access Programs Spur Growth. Urban Policy Briefing No. 99–2. Program in Politics and Policy, Michigan State University.

Hamlin, R. E. 2002. Public-Private Partnerships for Inner-City Revitalization. In C. S. Weissert, D.W. Thornton and A. M. Schneider, eds. *Urban Public Policy in Michigan.*

Hamlin, R. E., and F. S. Duma. 1999. The Capital Access Program: Its Application for Eastern Europe. *European Traditions and Experiences.* Ladislau Gyemant, ed. Cluj-Napoca: European Studies Foundation Publishing House.

Hamlin, R. E., and T. S. Lyons. 1996. *Economy without Walls: Managing Local Development in a Restructuring World.* New York: Praeger.

Lyons, T. S., and R. E. Hamlin. 2001. *Creating an Economic Development Action Plan: A Guide for Development Professionals*, Revised and Updated Edition. New York: Praeger.

Mahanty, A. K. 1980. *Intermediate Microeconomics with Applications.* New York: Academic Press.

Solomon, S. 1986. *Small Business USA: The Role of Small Companies in Sparking America's Economic Transformation.* New York: Crown Publishers.

Chapter 3

CURRENT APPROACHES TO DEBT-CAPITAL FORMATION: MICRO- AND DIRECT LENDING PROGRAMS

The first chapter of this book described the importance of small business development and success to society. Chapter 2 discussed the difficulty of channeling debt capital to existing and start-up small businesses, and the threat that problem poses for national economic development. Chapters 3 and 4 discuss in practical terms how government can and has increased the flow of small business debt capital.

Governments are involved in a wide variety of vehicles for lending to small businesses. In this chapter, two of these mechanisms are identified and discussed. These include micro-lending/microenterprise programs, and direct lending programs. These programs typically involve government or related agencies making loans directly to businesses. These are relatively higher risk situations, such as small start-up businesses. These businesses need small loans but would have little luck with conventional lenders. If government feels these situations are important, then plugging the debt capital gap directly is one public sector alternative.

Following this chapter, Chapter 4 discusses four mechanisms government can use to leverage private capital by indirectly inducing conventional lenders and other investors to participate in midrisk lending. Four programs discussed include loan guarantees, loan insurance pooling, loans with kicker features, and subordinated lending. These programs generally serve relatively less risky, more established companies and entrepreneurs and less risky situations. These entrepreneurs and situations are sometimes referred to as "almost bankable." As a result, inducing private capital to flow to them using risk-sharing incentives is more viable.

Each of the concepts and programs in these two chapters represents a unique approach to debt capital formation, with its own culture, goals, and procedures. In each case, the respective chapter delineates the concept and its theoretical underpinnings. It describes in detail how an example program works and then critiques the program. Once each of these vehicles is examined individually, an analysis of their collective shortcomings is presented at the end of Chapter 4.

MICRO-LENDING/MICROENTERPRISE PROGRAMS

The Concept

Micro-lending is targeted at low-income entrepreneurs who operate very small businesses that are considered too risky for traditional bank loans. These microentrepreneurs are unwilling and often unable to take on large amounts of debt. They are also unable to pay market rates of interest and put up standard collateral. Micro-loans provide their businesses with very small debt capital infusions, with minimal interest and collateral requirements.

In addition, most micro-loan programs in the U.S. are attached to a program for providing business management and technical assistance. This is in recognition of the fact that merely making capital available to entrepreneurs does not ensure business success.

Micro-lending and microenterprise development have an important role to play in capital provision. They operate at the lowest rung of the capital assistance ladder. They prepare high-risk entrepreneurs for managing traditional bank loans and, ultimately, for effectively utilizing equity capital. By acting as a portal through which low-income entrepreneurs can enter the community economy, they represent an ideal connection between community development and economic development (Lyons and Hamlin 2001). In this way, they lend themselves to government intervention because they are providing a service that is not offered in the free market to business people who are underserved.

The Government Program: History and Purpose

The origins of micro-lending in the United States are typically attributed to the Grameen Bank of Bangladesh. This was a community economic development effort to help very poor individuals, particularly women, to become self-sufficient through operating their own businesses. Under the Grameen model, very small loans are made to impoverished entrepreneurs. Peer groups, who, among their other duties, keep pressure on individual loan recipients to repay their debts, manage these loans.

In the United States economy, micro-loan sizes are substantially greater than they are in the developing world. Nevertheless, they are small by American standards, being typically $25,000 or less. While pure micro-lending programs still exist in the United States, it has become evident that merely lending money to economically disadvantaged entrepreneurs will not ensure their success. Thus, most programs are now microenterprise programs, which consist of both a micro-lending program and a technical training program. Technical training is a term used to describe classroom teaching and one-on-one coaching in either the technical aspects of how to produce a particular product or service or in how to operate a business on a day-to-day basis.

Microenterprise programs in the United States emerged in the 1980s with several pioneer programs. ACCION International (which has six U.S. offices), Working Capital of Boston, and the Good Faith Fund of Arkansas all were early American versions of the Grameen model. A number of community action agencies (e.g., Central Vermont Community Action Council) and community development corporations added microenterprise programs to their activities during this time. Microenterprise development also became popular as a vehicle for helping individuals, particularly women, to transition from welfare to self-sufficiency. The Women's Economic Development Corporation of St. Paul, Minnesota, was one of the first organizations to recognize that job training for employment in corporations will not provide employment for all welfare recipients who need a job. Preparation for self-employment must also be an option. This idea was extended to the wider welfare population by pilot projects launched by the U.S. Department of Labor and the Corporation for Enterprise Development in the late 1980s (Aspen Institute 2000a).

Microenterprise development continued to grow in the United States throughout the 1990s and into the Twenty-first Century. These programs have become part of the activities of such varied organizations as housing and social service programs, credit unions, community colleges, rural policy centers, and refugee resettlement programs, among others (Aspen Institute 2000a). Microenterprise development practitioners now have their own professional organization: the Association for Economic Opportunity (AEO).

MICROENTERPRISE PROGRAM: HOW THE PROGRAM WORKS

In recent years, the focus of microenterprise programs has shifted dramatically away from lending toward technical assistance. A study conducted in the late 1990s revealed that only 11 percent of the 55,756 microentrepreneurs served by U.S. programs were borrowers. The rest utilize only training and technical services (Langer, Orwick and Kays 1999). Despite this, micro-lending remains an important early stage type of capital formation in the United States.

Micro-loans are intended for entrepreneurs who are unable to obtain debt capital from traditional lending sources. Furthermore, these entrepreneurs are typically low income and face what Lichtenstein and Lyons (1996) call "transaction barriers"—problems with the actual exchange in obtaining a loan—because they are women or members of minority groups. For these reasons, they require loans that:

- They can compete for on a level playing field;
- Are small enough to be manageable;
- Carry below-market interest rates;
- Are of a reasonable term; and
- Have minimal collateral requirements (Aspen Institute 2000b).

There are two types of micro-lending: individual lending and peer group lending. While some micro-lending organizations specialize in one or the other, some programs, like Business Plus in inner-city Louisville, Kentucky, utilize both approaches. Individual lending is the newer approach. It is the result of dissatisfaction on the part of some micro-lenders with the sometimes-cumbersome nature of peer lending. The transaction in individual lending is directly between the lender and the borrower, or the borrower's business. A microentrepreneur seeking a loan applies to the lending organization. A loan committee typically makes lending decisions; although, in some instances, the micro-lender's staff or board of advisers/directors plays this role. Most loans serve as seed capital or working capital for the borrowing business. As micro-lenders have become more sophisticated, they have become better able to be more flexible in their collateral requirements and loan sizes, allowing them to continue to serve their low-income clientele in a way that is more relevant to today's business climate (Aspen Institute 2000b).

In peer lending, the loan is made by the micro-lender to an established group of peer entrepreneurs. This group often screens its own members for eligibility and typically manages the repayment of loans. The underlying theory, of course, is that peer pressure will help to ensure timely loan repayment. This is reinforced by the fact that, in most programs, default by one member will preclude others in the group access to loans. Some programs even have forced savings requirements for their peer lending group members as a way of hedging against defaults. Other programs require a minimum number of hours of technical training or the borrower will be considered to be in default. On the other hand, timely loan repayment can result in additional, and larger, loans for the group member (Aspen 2000b).

Today, peer lending is no longer the predominant form of micro-lending. Individual lending has assumed that mantle. A study by the Aspen Institute found that 65 percent of micro-lending organizations make individual loans, 16 percent use peer lending systems, while 10 percent utilize both (Aspen 2000b).

Funding for microenterprise programs has come from a variety of sources, often in combination. It has been estimated that the federal government, alone, invested over $300 million in microenterprise development in the 1990s (Else 1999). Among the federal agencies involved were the departments of Agriculture, Health and Human Services, Housing and Urban Development, Labor, Treasury, and the Small Business Administration, as well as the Appalachian Regional Commission. HUD's Community Development Block Grant (CDBG) funds are particularly widely used by local microenterprise programs (Aspen Institute 2000c).

Some state agencies also support microenterprise development. They do so using several vehicles, including acting as a pass through for CDBG money, using earned income tax money, and drawing on general funds. Some states have used Temporary Assistance for Needy Families (TANF) funds as well; however, this money is time constrained and tends to be used more for job-placement efforts (Aspen Institute 2000c).

As noted above, lending has become a secondary activity for microenterprise development organizations. The greatest volume of their work is now technical training. While a few microenterprise programs around the country still do a good loan volume, on average, such programs make only twenty-four loans per year (Aspen 2000c).

The principal reasons behind this relatively low volume of loans are three-fold. First, most of the prospective clients of these programs are low income. This causes them to be very leery of borrowing money. Second, it is often faster and easier to obtain money using family, friends, or credit cards. Finally, the lending products available through microenterprise programs are often very limited, making them less relevant to the needs of microentrepreneurs. Many prospective clients are looking elsewhere (Aspen 2000c).

This bit of irony is not lost on the micro-lenders. With the help of the Microenterprise Fund for Innovation, Effectiveness, Learning and Dissemination (FIELD), they are experimenting with new products and procedures designed to better fit the needs of microentrepreneurs. One such line of products permits the conversion of debt capital to internal equity. An example is West CAP's "Business Investment Trust" accounts. These allow the borrower to place 40 percent of the loan payments in an escrow account. After repaying the loan on time for twelve months, the borrower can access this money and use it for purchasing equipment and inventory, improving property, or as working capital. Another group of loan products is aimed at niche markets among microentrepreneurs. Thus, loans are tailored to food processors, day-care providers, and craft makers, to name a few. New loan products are also aimed at assisting business loan customers with their personal finances. The thinking here is that if these folks' personal finances are in order, they are unlikely to negatively impact their businesses' finances. Finally, some micro-lenders now experiment with loans for large peer groups, featuring enhanced underwriting that lowers collateral requirements (Aspen 2000c).

Micro-lenders also try to reach more prospective clients by enhancing their lending procedures. They market their loan programs more aggressively and back their practices with market research. They are taking a greater burden off the shoulders of their loan officers by engaging in loan processing by "back shop" administrative offices, where possible, and by increasing the efficiency of underwriting processes through the adoption of credit scoring systems. They are also experimenting with new lines of credit to organizations with established constituencies, such as local economic development agencies and related trade associations (Aspen 2000c).

Because microenterprise programs vary so much in their specific missions and structures, it is difficult to delineate a prototypical program. It may be useful to describe a successful program as an example. The Business Plus Microenterprise Program operates in the economically disadvantaged neighborhoods of the west side of Louisville, Kentucky. It was the first comprehensive microenterprise program established in that state. Its clients are principally low-income and African American, and predominately women (Durr, Lyons and Cornwell 1998).

Unlike many microenterprise programs, Business Plus did not begin as a micro-loan program. Instead, it started in 1992 as a training program for business plan development, which was the forerunner of the present-day

Business Plus Training Institute. In 1994, Business Plus began developing its micro-lending capacity with a $25,000 grant from the Louisville-Jefferson County Office for Economic Development, the local public economic development agency at that time. This permitted Business Plus to create its Micro-Loan Program. Thus, Business Plus has developed separate business and technical training and micro-lending divisions within its organization which it has linked in appropriate ways (Durr, Lyons and Cornwell 1998).

The Training Institute is designed to deliver business skill development and technical training in a group-oriented, supportive environment. Using a framework created by Lichtenstein and Lyons (1996), Business Plus assesses its clients' entrepreneurial skills upon entering the program, which, in turn, permits the program to track each client into a strategic and appropriate training regimen. Training is provided in a comprehensive array of business subjects: marketing, management, accounting/bookkeeping, strategic planning, etc. While some of the instruction is conducted by Business Plus staff, most of it is offered by volunteer professionals from the community. Strong interaction among clients, staff, and volunteers is encouraged in order to provide the training in an emotionally supportive environment (Durr, Lyons, and Cornwell 1998). This approach builds social capital within the microenterprise program and a bridge from dependence to independence. A large number of the Training Institute's clients are not Business Plus borrowers. They are merely availing themselves of the training opportunity. Those who are receiving micro-loans, however, must honor their commitment to a specified minimum of 40 hours of training or they will be considered in default on their loans.

The micro-lending side of Business Plus' house made its first loans in 1994. Originally, the Grameen, peer-lending model was employed exclusively. Under this model, clients are placed in small (peer) groups of four to seven. A revolving loan fund of $10,000 is established for each group. The peer group is made responsible for activities that included client screening, loan application review, loan repayment collection, and technical assistance (Durr, Lyons, and Cornwell 1998). The ability of each client to obtain additional and/or larger loans is based on the overall credit performance of the peer group, bringing peer pressure to bear on everyone for complete and timely loan repayment. No Business Plus client is eligible to obtain a loan until he or she has completed a business plan and has formally committed to taking 40 hours of training, as described above. Peer groups make one or two loans at a time. When it is demonstrated that these loans are being repaid in a timely manner, additional loans to peer group members are made (Durr, Lyons, and Cornwell 1998). As one might imagine, given the small loan fund, peer group loans are quite small.

When Business Plus received a $250,000 grant from the U.S. Small Business Administration's Micro-Loan Demonstration Program, the microenterprise program was able to provide direct lending as a second option for clients. Under direct lending, the program makes loans directly to the micro-entrepreneur without the peer group apparatus. These loans range from $5,000 up to $25,000. The requirements for loan eligibility are similar to those for the peer lending program. The Business Plus Loan Review Committee, made up of community volunteers, reviews each loan application and evaluates it based on established criteria. Rejected applications are accompanied by very specific descriptions of their shortcomings, and applicants are given the opportunity to correct these deficiencies and resubmit them (Durr, Lyons, and Cornwell 1998).

While direct lending can be very effective in and of itself, Business Plus has recognized the benefits of peer group interaction and has initiated a program that provides these latter advantages to its direct lendees. The Industry Growth Groups (IGG) program is aimed at bringing together micro-entrepreneurs in the same industry to engage in networking activities that permit idea-sharing, the pooling of resources, and the joint pursuit of market opportunities, among others. Business Plus has developed IGGs in business services, commercial and construction contracting, fine art/folk art, personal and salon services, and specialized retail. Groups have also been created around functional activities, such as financial management, human resources, investment, marketing, and technology. In order to encourage participation in IGGs, Business Plus allows its lendees to count their participation toward the established training requirements.

In the late 1990's, the Business Plus program management began noticing a troubling phenomenon. A number of their client businesses that had passed the start-up stage were floundering. These businesses seemed to have reached a plateau in their development and could go no further. The entrepreneurs involved had been in business for a period ranging from three years to eleven years.

The management realized that, while Business Plus was very successful in working with businesses in the start-up phase, they lacked the capacity to help entrepreneurs who had advanced beyond this level. These entrepreneurs were facing a new set of higher order challenges that they were not prepared to address. The entrepreneurs were not aware of where else in the community to turn for help, nor was Business Plus.

Ultimately, Business Plus entered into a partnership with the University of Louisville's College of Business and Public Administration Together they sought a grant from the Coleman Foundation to develop a new training program that was tailored to the needs of these post-start-up entrepreneurs. The partners were successful in obtaining a grant from Coleman, which was used to assess the needs of the entrepreneurs and design a training curriculum to fit those needs. In particular, they determined that there was a need for skill development in the areas of industry research, strategic planning, marketing, managing people, use of computers, and operations planning and management. While the training appears to have helped these entrepreneurs, finding funding to continue this program of training for future Business Plus clients has proven difficult. Business Plus has begun to look to other business assistance providers in the community to help with clients who have moved past the start-up phase in their business's evolution.

This situation serves as an example of two important themes of this book. The first is that capital, alone, will not transform entrepreneurs or their businesses. Successful enterprise development must involve the melding of a variety of forms of assistance over a substantial time period. Second, no single entrepreneurship assistance provider is capable of fully developing all entrepreneurs and their businesses. Each provider has its own assets and limitations. If a community's enterprise development activities are to be successful, every provider must understand its place in that system and how to interact with other providers in relevant ways to ensure that the needs of local entrepreneurs are being met.

Evaluation of Micro-lending/Microenterprise Programs

Community Perspective

From the perspective of the community, micro-lending and microenterprise development offer innovative solutions to some of the needs of low-income entrepreneurs. By making capital available in "digestible chunks" and by supplementing that with assistance in effectively managing a business, these programs help to bootstrap small businesses that might otherwise have never gotten off the ground.

A longitudinal study by the Aspen Institute, conducted between 1991 and 1997, identified several measurable community outcomes attributable to microenterprise programs (Aspen Institute 2000a). This study found that the average household income for low-income clients increased by more than $10,500, while business assets increased by more than $18,700. At the conclusion of the study, Aspen found that 53 percent of these low-income clients had exited the poverty level. The survival rate of microenterprise program clients was determined to be 17 percent higher than that of small businesses in the general population. Finally, during the period of the study, the percentage of clients receiving public assistance dropped significantly.

Job creation is often the principal yardstick that government uses to measure economic development program success. On this dimension, microenterprise programs do not fare as well as some other debt capital initiatives. By their nature, microenterprises employ a small number of individuals. Many have only one to three employees. In terms of sheer numbers, their impact is often unimpressive. Nevertheless, they are providing a means of support to many people who might not otherwise be employed. Because their assistance is typically to start-ups, they are also helping many businesses to take the first step along the path of growth. As these businesses evolve, they tend to outgrow the help of microenterprise programs; thus, any employment growth that they experience may not redound directly to the credit of these programs. Nevertheless, microenterprise programs have played a key role in helping these businesses reach the level of growth and development they now enjoy.

Micro-Lender Perspective

In a 1994 study of seven microenterprise programs, the Aspen Institute concluded that the costs incurred by these programs in their activities compared favorably to those of other business development programs (Aspen Institute 2000a). Despite this, costs were still high, and rising (Langer, Orwick and Kays 1999). Aspen found that the average cost per client in 1994 was $1,707 ($2,535 for a welfare client); the average cost per job created or retained was $5,813; the average cost per assisted business was $3,018; and the average cost to make and manage a loan was about $1.50 per dollar loaned (Edgcomb, Klein and Clark 1996).

In micro-lending, as in other enterprise development programs, a new emphasis on a program's financial self-sufficiency has emerged. Therefore, programs are striving to achieve break-even status. A 1998 study of five micro-lending programs revealed that two of these programs were more than paying for themselves. On average, the programs were covering 75.5 percent of their costs (Aspen Institute 2000b). Despite progress, studies show that micro-lending programs are struggling with loan default problems. In the late 1990s, portfolio at-risk rates ranged from 6 percent up to 40 percent, indicating substantial unevenness (Aspen 2000b).

In programs that focus on training, the cost of making and managing loans is higher. This is to be expected as a result of lower lending volume. Interestingly, only 48 percent of the clients of training-led programs actually have businesses, as opposed to 100 percent of clients of lending-led programs. Nevertheless, a higher percentage of training-led programs' loans go to start-up businesses, and these programs make more loans to low-income clients (Aspen 2000b).

Small Business Client Perspective

From the perspective of clients, microenterprise development programs have their advantages and their disadvantages. On the positive side, these programs provide debt capital that is affordable to entrepreneurs who often cannot access such capital anywhere else. When this capital is offered in tandem with business management and technical training, it can provide an invaluable "leg up" for individuals who are new to entrepreneurship, especially those who are low income. This makes such programs especially useful to people who are victims of corporate downsizing or who are being moved from the welfare rolls to work, in the form of self-employment.

On the negative side, while microenterprise programs can be very helpful in the early stages of entrepreneurship and business development, their utility drops off dramatically as small companies move from the start-up phase to higher levels of development. The loan sizes are no longer adequate to meet capital needs, and the technical assistance is no longer at a level necessary to help entrepreneurs to build the skills required to meet the emerging challenges they face. Yet, many programs fail to recognize this, clinging to their clients long after start-up and causing them to stagnate and to become overly dependent (Lyons 2001).

As noted above, the volume of micro-loans has dropped off, with more attention being paid to business and technical training. This is in part because many microentrepreneurs are unwilling to take on debt from a source outside their own circle of family and friends. It also stems from a sometimes-true perception on the part of prospective clients that the way that micro-loans are currently structured does not fit their needs.

Summary

Although microenterprise programs probably do a better job of nurturing client enterprises, particularly start-ups, than do any other type of

enterprise development program, they are incapable of completely transforming entrepreneurs alone. They provide a good starting place on the
journey to successful entrepreneurship by giving their clients the opportunity to launch their businesses and prove that they can effectively manage
capital.

DIRECT GOVERNMENT LENDING

The Concept

As the name implies, direct government lending involves loans that are
made by governments (particularly local governments) directly to businesses for economic development purposes. These are most often loans
made to small businesses because they are typically underserved by traditional lenders, due to the perceived risk involved. Thus, government only
gets involved in direct lending when no one else will, and when the success of the business is consequential to the community's well-being (Hamlin and Lyons 1996).

The Government Program

The principal type of direct lending to small businesses by local government is through a revolving loan fund (RLF). Revolving loan funds
take their name from the fact that as loans are re-paid, the principal is
returned to the fund to be lent to another small business. Some revolving
loan funds lend at below-market interest rates. Others lend at market rates
of interest. This is dependent upon the mission of the fund. Typically,
interest and loan processing fees are used to pay for the RLF's administration (Hamlin and Lyons 1996).

Three broad classifications of revolving loan funds are distinguished by
the nature of their funding (Singer 2000):

Capitalized RLF: A capitalized RLF is one that has a permanent funding
source. Typically, these RLFs face no requirement that the money has to
be paid back to the source. Capitalized RLFs are the preferred structure for
such funds for these reasons. Sources of capital for these funds can be public (at any of the three levels of government) or private. Private sources
may include corporations, foundations, or wealthy individuals.

Soft Loan RLF: In this RLF structure, the funding source(s) loan the
capital to the fund with an expectation that it will be repaid. This loan is
made at below-market interest rates, making it a "soft" loan. This is obviously a less desirable situation for the organization managing the RLF, as

it puts greater pressure on them to ensure that the loans they make from the fund are paid back, and that this happens in a timely manner.

Debt Capital RLF: The least desirable funding structure for an RLF is the debt capital approach. Under this structure, capital for the fund is acquired by borrowing it at market rates of interest. This makes operating the RLF more expensive which, in turn, can make borrowing from the fund more onerous. Operators of such funds often find that they must be more creative in their lending and management practices in order to meet their clients' needs. The size of loans, interest, and collateral requirements will vary with the type of RLF, its clientele, its location, and its mission.

Revolving loan funds may be operated by a wide variety of organizations. Some are managed by government economic development agencies. Others are operated by not-for-profit economic development organizations created for that purpose. Still others are housed in Community Development Corporations (CDCs), some of these operated by faith-based organizations. In Ephraim, Utah, the RLF was established and is operated by a regional association of governments (Lyons, Lichtenstein and Chhatre 1999).

The Revolving Loan Fund Program sponsored by the U.S. Economic Development Administration (EDA) is a good example of federal level involvement in this type of direct government lending. The EDA's program focuses on providing initial capital to locally based RLFs that are managed by not-for-profit corporations. The purpose of the creation of these revolving loan funds is to encourage business and job creation and retention and to facilitate the development of new high technology industries (Bingaman 2002).

The EDA's program was initiated in 1976. Since that time, it has provided capital to more than 480 local funds. The local funds have made well over 7,000 loans, leveraging almost $2 billion in private capital (Bingaman 2002).

Some RLFs are very focused in their purpose. An example of such a fund is the Empower Baltimore Brownfields Loan and Grant Program, created in 1997. This program seeks to encourage the redevelopment of the city's brownfields by providing below-market loans to be used in buying land, conducting environmental assessments, undertaking environmental clean-up efforts, and paying for environmental insurance. The loans have a term ranging from two to five years. Each loan covers between 10 and 50 percent of total costs, with the hope that this can be used to leverage additional private investment in the project. In its first eighteen months, the program made five loans that ranged in size from $150,000 to $340,000 (Singer 2000).

Evaluation of the Program

Community Perspective

From a community perspective, revolving loan funds can be very beneficial. They offer debt capital for start-up and operating expenses to entrepreneurs who may not otherwise have access to this capital, particularly from traditional sources. They do this by helping certain entrepreneurs overcome the obstacles they face in acquiring debt capital. RLFs make debt capital affordable by reducing the interest and collateral burdens. They also help entrepreneurs overcome certain transaction barriers to obtaining capital, including poor credit, gender bias, racism, and so forth (Lichtenstein and Lyons 1996). They do this by being flexible and open in their lending practices.

When these obstacles are addressed and removed, it helps bring entrepreneurship and self-employment within reach for a larger group of individuals in the community. This, in turn, creates jobs and helps diversify the local economy. Furthermore, it serves to perfect the market for capital by intervening to bring entrepreneurs into that market who would, otherwise, be permanently left out.

All of this is accomplished at little or no cost to the entities that operate RLFs, assuming they avoid bad loans. The biggest expense is in putting together the money for the base fund. Because of its revolving nature, the fund then replenishes itself. Fees help cover administrative costs. Money for the base fund need not come directly from the RLF operating organization, either. It can be raised from a variety of sources and under several different structures, as discussed above.

Lender Organization Perspective

The lender organization's perspective on the RLF will vary depending upon the type of fund structure being utilized. A capitalized RLF removes the stress of constantly pursuing money to keep the fund afloat. Soft loan and debt capital RLFs require substantial time and effort on the part of the fund operator.

Another major concern for the lender is default. RLFs can ill afford defaults on payment of the loans they make, as this cuts into the base fund. Therefore careful management of the loan portfolio is essential. This situation is exacerbated by the fact that borrowers from these funds tend to be higher risk, which is, of course, why they are not currently bankable. Furthermore, the loan officer or committee must make loan decisions without the help of natural market forces or bank expertise. When making a direct, first position loan, they are on their own. The decision is in their lap. They must not only understand small business lending but also know the prospective borrower well. They should also be familiar with the industry and market in which each business participates. This is a difficult job for an organization that is often operated by public employees and volunteers.

Borrower Perspective

For RLF borrowers, these funds may well represent the only hope for acquiring capital for their businesses. This makes the RLF a most welcome resource in the community. However, this should not be taken to suggest that borrowing entrepreneurs are universally pleased with RLFs. Koven and Lyons (2003) tell of the entrepreneur in rural Wisconsin who lamented that the revolving loan fund operated by the local business incubator was only able to loan him enough money to put him out of business. That is, the loans were large enough to help get his business started, but not enough to provide the working capital to keep it going in its early years. This speaks to another limitation of revolving loan funds—they cannot be the sole source of financing for any business and should not be expected to play that role. Instead, RLFs must be understood as merely one source of financial capital among many, with a very specific role to play. They provide debt capital to start-up and very-early-stage companies that have not yet proven that they can effectively manage such capital. They are a source of limited capital *and* a proving ground on the way to bankability.

All of the above-described benefits and cautions emphasize that, to succeed, revolving loan funds must be well networked with a community's larger enterprise development system, including other small business service providers, lenders, educators, planners, and other small businesses. They must tap expertise from throughout the community both formally and informally to raise initial capital, avoid bad loan decisions, and help businesses succeed.

REFERENCES

Aspen Institute. 2000a. *Microenterprise Development in the United States: An Overview,* Microenterprise Fact Sheet Series 1. Washington, D.C.: Microenterprise Fund for Innovation, Effectiveness, Learning and Dissemination (FIELD), Aspen Institute.

Aspen Institute. 2000b. *Business Capital for Microentrepreneurs: Providing Microloans,* Microenterprise Fact Sheet Series 3. Washington, D.C.: Micro-enterprise Fund for Innovation, Effectiveness, Learning and Dissemination (FIELD), Aspen Institute.

Aspen Institute. 2000c. *Sources of Public Funding,* Microenterprise Fact Sheet Series 5. Washington, D.C.: Microenterprise Fund for Innovation, Effec-tiveness, Learning and Dissemination (FIELD), Aspen Institute.

Bingaman, J. 2002. Senator Jeff Bingaman's Small Business Resource Guide. http://www.senate.gov/~bingaman/sb/html/edaloan.html.

Durr, M., T. S. Lyons, and K. K. Cornwell. 1998. Social Cost and Enterprise Development within African American Communities. *National Journal of Sociology,* 12: 57–77.

Edgcomb, E., J. Klein, and P. Clark. 1996. *The Practice of Microenterprise in the U.S.: Strategies, Costs and Effectiveness.* Washington, D.C.: The Self-Employment Learning Project, The Aspen Institute.

Else, J. 1999. *Overview of the Microenterprise Development Field in the U.S.* Geneva: ILO.

Friedman, R., and P. Sahay. 1996. Six Steps Forward for Microenterprise Devel-opment in the United States. *Entrepreneurial Economy Review,* 32–37.

Hamlin, R. E., and T. S. Lyons. 1996. *Economy Without Walls: Managing Local Development in a Restructuring World.* Westport, CT: Praeger.

Koven, S. G., and T. S. Lyons. 2003. *Economic Development: Strategies for State and Local Practice.* Washington, D.C.: International City/County Manage-ment Association.

Langer, J., J. Orwick, and A. Kays. 1999. *1999 Directory of U.S. Microenterprise Programs.* Washington, D.C.: The Aspen Institute.

Lichtenstein, G..A. and T. S. Lyons. 1996. *Incubating New Enterprises: A Guide to Successful Practice.* Washington, D.C.: The Aspen Institute.

Lyons, T. S. 2002. *The Entrepreneurial League System®: Transforming Your Community's Economy Through Enterprise Development.* Washington, D.C.: The Appalachian Regional Commission.

Lyons, T. S. 2001. *Articulating the Current Minority Business Development Sys-tem in Louisville, Kentucky.* Louisville: Center for Research on Entrepre-neurship and Enterprise Development, College of Business and Public Administration, University of Louisville.

Lyons, T. S.. and R. E. Hamlin. 2001. *Creating an Economic Development Action Plan: A Guide for Development Professionals,* Revised and Updated Edi-tion. Westport, CT: Praeger.

Lyons, T. S., G. A. Lichtenstein, and S. Chhatre. 1999. Assessing the Efficacy of Rural Business Incubation: A Diagnostic Approach from the United States." *Journal of Rural Development,* 18, 1: 29–49.

Oliver, M. L., and T. M. Shapiro. 1997. *Black Wealth/White Wealth: A New Perspective on Racial Inequality.* New York: Routledge.

Rahman, A. 1999. Women and Microcredit in Rural Bangladesh: An Anthropological Study of Grameen Bank Lending. Boulder, CO: Westview Press.

Scheer, K., and J. Reynolds. 1999. The Future of Microenterprise Development: What are the Challenges? *Rural Enterprise Reporter,* September, 17:1.

Singer. 2000. "Revolving Loan Funds: It Seemed Like a Simple Plan." *Public Management* 82, 11: A3-A14 (Special Section).

Chapter 4

INDIRECT APPROACHES TO LEVERAGING PRIVATE CAPITAL

The approach described in Chapter 3 is for government to fill gaps in the debt capital markets by making loans directly to businesses, typically through some other institution such as an authority or non-governmental organization. Another approach is to use governmental powers and resources to leverage more private capital (particularly from banks) into midrisk small business lending. This approach might be preferable because: (1) it expands the resources flowing to small businesses; (2) it removes government from the management and oversight of business operations; (3) by requiring private lender or investor participation, private capital is not crowded out of a market that might be served without government involvement; and (4) if done properly, such an approach might build intermediary institutions, strengthen market mechanisms, and greatly expand midrisk capital investment over time. To accomplish these goals government must lower the risk for private capitalists to participate in the midrisk market so that risks are commensurate with perceived rewards. This typically involves some government risk sharing. Four public/ private partnership approaches discussed in this chapter are loan guarantees, loan insurance, loan kicker mechanisms, and subordinated lending. Governmental programs using these approaches are described and critiqued. Once each of these vehicles is examined individually, an analysis of the collective shortcomings of current governmental interventions is presented at the end of the chapter.

LOAN GUARANTEE PROGRAMS

The Concept

Since government may prefer to induce capital markets to provide midrisk capital formation rather than be the supplier of capital, approaches that leverage private capital are often preferred. One approach that has existed for decades is to have government provide a partial guarantee of a private loan. As its name implies, the loan guarantee involves the government making a promise to the private lender that should the loan recipient default, the government will reimburse the lending institution for a portion of its loss. This means that if a borrower fails financially and a loan becomes non performing, the bank will go through the collection and recovery process. Then the governmental agency providing the guarantee will pay the lender for the amount not recovered, up to the level of the guarantee. This promise frees the private lender to make small business loans that it might not otherwise have made.

Risk sharing is critical to the market perfection process. In the case of the guaranteed loan, the borrower is at risk if a down payment or business equity contribution to the financed project is required; the lender is at risk for that part of the loan that is not guaranteed, and the guarantor is at risk for the guaranteed portion. The tax-paying public is at risk if the guarantor is a government agency using budgeted funds. In this way risk is shared among all that also stand to benefit. The small business owner is rewarded if the loan leads to greater business success. The lender earns loan interest and gains from a variety of less tangible benefits; and the community experiences the advantages of greater economic growth with concomitant employment gains, tax-base enhancement, and reduction of social problems associated with unemployment and poverty. The program works and becomes a win-win situation if the perceived risk faced by each party matches the perceived reward.

Keeping overall risk as low as possible is obviously important to make the process work. That requires good analysis of and assistance to businesses. Assistance helps to ensure the success of borrowers and minimize the number of times that loan losses are taken by stakeholders. Program success also requires keeping processing and servicing costs to a minimum for all parties. Distribution of risk is also important and is dependent on (1) the level of down payment required and (2) the amount of the loan that is guaranteed. Finding the proper balance concerning these parameters is the secret recipe. If so, everyone will want to come to the table.

Governments at all levels can and do use the loan guarantee concept. A local revolving loan fund, for example, can use its pool as backing for a guarantee program instead of or in addition to a loan program. In some states organizations with tax increment financing (TIF) powers, such as downtown development authorities, tax increment finance authorities or brownfield redevelopment authorities, may use the funds generated by the tax increment to back bank loans with guarantees. If carefully and successfully carried out, the guarantee process will cost the tax increment agency very little while drawing private debt capital into the community. If the loan creates a successful small business, then the increase in property values caused by the new development will increase the annual contribution to the tax increment. In these situations the taxpayer experiences little risk unless multiple loan failures endanger the integrity of the increment fund.

Local economic development agencies that use loan guarantees must remember that they need to replenish the fund in anticipation of some loan losses and administrative expenses. In a loan guarantee program a fee is typically charged to the business for the right to receive a guarantee.

SBA Loan Guarantee Programs: History and Purpose

Because of regulatory restrictions and obligations to shareholders, private banks must be very cautious when lending to small businesses. Many of these businesses are perceived as being almost bankable, but not quite. If these businesses had the opportunity to demonstrate that they could manage debt capital, they might very well become attractive to private lenders. One way to help these companies overcome this obstacle is to reduce the risk to the private bank of making the loan. The federal government, through its Small Business Administration, has been doing precisely that for many years. The SBA's primary mechanism for reducing risk to private lenders is the loan guarantee.

Since the creation of the U.S. Small Business Administration in 1953 the U.S. Government has attempted to diversify the intermediary system by employing a variety of investment vehicles, including loan guarantees, to channel debt capital to small businesses. In particular, the U.S. Small Business Administration (SBA) has attempted to promote medium-risk lending to small businesses through the SBA's 7(a) Loan Guaranty Program from nearly the inception of the agency. Almost 50 years later this continues to be the SBA's primary business loan program. The 7(a) general loan guaranty program represents 90 percent of the agency's total loan effort. Between 1980 and 1990 SBA provided guarantees for 180,000 loans worth more than $31 billion (CCH 2002).

Generally speaking, the SBA guarantees up to 85 percent of the loss due to default on loans of $150,000 or less. For loans over $150,000, the guarantee is for 75 percent of the loss. In most cases, the guarantee is capped at $1 million. The SBA does ask lenders to certify that they could not have made the loan without the guarantee and that small business borrowers meet the SBA's eligibility criteria.

Most often, an SBA guarantee is sought when a conventional lender finds that the prospective borrower has insufficient collateral to support the loan request. From the lender's point of view, the SBA loan guarantee works as a substitute for the needed collateral and provides the lender with satisfactory security to support the loan (CCH 2002).

Over the years 7(a) has evolved with the addition of subsidiary programs to serve a variety of small business financing needs. One of the programs is a loan guarantee pre-qualification mechanism while others are spin-off loan guarantee programs with different rules. Some of these programs are the Pre-qualification Loan Program, the Low Doc Program, SBAExpress, CAPlines, Export Working Capital Program, and the International Trade Loan Program.

How the Programs Work

SBA 7(a) Loan Guaranty Program

SBA's primary loan guaranty program is the 7(a) program, which derives its name from the section number of the legislation that created it. It is a basic loan guarantee of the type described above. Loans are made to small businesses by private lenders, which are, in turn, backed by the SBA.

Loan and Guarantee Amount. Effective December 22, 2000, a maximum loan amount of $2 million was established for 7(a) loans and the maximum amount to be guaranteed by the SBA was set at $1 million for most situations. Small loans (those under $150,000) carry a maximum guarantee of 85 percent.

Maturities. Maturity periods vary depending upon how the loan is used, the estimated economic life of the assets being financed and the applicant's ability to repay. Maturities on 7(a) loans can extend to ten years for working capital and twenty-five years for fixed assets.

The following maximum maturities apply for loans with different purposes:

- working capital: seven to ten years;
- machinery and equipment: ten to fifteen years; or,
- building purchase or construction: twenty-five years.

When loan proceeds are used for a combination of purposes, the maximum maturity is a weighted average of the corresponding maximums.

Most small businesses have considerable difficulty obtaining long-term financing, because small business lending is so risky. A claimed benefit of a SBA loan guarantee is that the government's backing induces or allows lenders to provide a longer-term loan. Instead of three- to five-year maximums on conventional bank loans for a small business, sometimes with balloons, the SBA guarantee may induce loans up to twenty-five years. These longer terms provide much-needed cash flow consistency. Regular 7(a) guarantees also prohibit the use of balloon payments or prepayment penalties (CCH 2002).

Interest Rate and Fees. The interest rate charged by banks for guaranteed loans may, within certain limits, reflect prevailing market rates. Interest charges may also either be fixed over the life of the loan or fluctuate with the market. While interest rates on 7(a) loans can be negotiated between lenders and borrowing businesses, the SBA has set maximums for fixed rate loans based on loan amount and maturity period. These maximums are stated as a fixed number of percentage points above New York prime as reported in the *Wall Street Journal*. These maximums are as follows:

Loan Amount	Maturity Period	Maximum Interest Rate
$50,000 or more	less than 7 years	Prime + 2.25%
$50,000 or more	7 years or more	Prime + 2.75%
$25,000-$50,000	less than 7 years	Prime + 3.25%
$25,000-$50,000	7 years or more	Prime + 3.75%
$25,000 or less	less than 7 years	Prime + 4.25%
$25,000 or less	7 years or more	Prime + 4.75%

If the lender uses a floating rate, the rate can be adjusted periodically pursuant to the guarantee agreement with the SBA; however, the spread between an adjusted rate and New York prime cannot be increased.

The maximum rate schedule generally allows certified, private lenders to charge a slightly higher interest rate for an SBA-guaranteed loan than for a similar conventional loan so as to induce private lenders to be involved. Also, loans under $50,000 can carry even higher interest rates so that private lenders have an incentive to make such small loans. The SBA previously sponsored a Small Loan Program for these small loans, but that program has been incorporated into the LowDoc program discussed later. The maximum interest schedule also gives private lenders some incentive to extend the maturity of a loan (CCH 2002). The SBA's guarantee fee of

2 percent to 3.875 percent of the loan amount may be passed on to the borrower for small loans.

While interest rates and additional costs sometimes make an SBA-guaranteed loan more expensive for the borrower than a conventional loan, one must consider counterbalancing factors. For one, the SBA prohibits extraneous fees. If the bank were to make the loan without the SBA guarantee, the lender might assess additional up-front points because of the higher risk; these points could equal the SBA guarantee fee. In contrast, SBA loans prohibit points from being assessed in addition to the guarantee fee (CCH 2002).

Security for the Loan. Part of the purpose of the loan guarantee program is to offset dependence on the effects of collateral-oriented lending by banks. Therefore, the SBA claims that when considering a business's application for a 7(a) loan, the SBA looks first to the prospective borrower's cash flow as it pertains to his or her ability to repay the loan. Attention is also paid to such factors as the character of the borrower, the entrepreneur's business management experience and capability, credit worthiness, the owner's equity contribution, collateral, and proof of sufficient commitment to the business. Weaknesses in one area may be balanced by strength in other areas.

Stated SBA policy is that a guarantee will not be denied merely because of inadequate collateral. Yet, in most instances, the private lender will still demand collateral, and the SBA's guarantee of an under-collateralized loan will be extended only if the business exhibits other favorable factors to support the creditworthiness of the borrower. The most important collateral consideration for the SBA is whether the loan is collateralized to the maximum capability of the individual business owner. An owner who has valuable personal assets might be requested to pledge those assets as security on the loan before the SBA would agree to take the risk of guaranteeing it. Unlike some of the other loan security requirements, a personal guarantee by all owners having at least a 20 percent interest in the company is usually nonnegotiable (CCH 2002).

Use of Proceeds. Loan proceeds from a 7(a) guaranteed loan may be used to establish a new business or to assist in the operation, acquisition or expansion of an existing business. Borrowers are permitted to use a 7(a) loan for a variety of purposes. These include real estate purchase, if the business will be located at that site; construction costs; renovation costs; equipment, machinery, furniture and fixtures purchases; inventory purchases; and working capital. Under no circumstances may the borrower use the loan to purchase real estate chiefly for investment purposes, pay delinquent taxes, finance floor plans, or refinance debt (unless such refinancing will benefit the business and was not made necessary by mismanagement).

Required Owner's Equity. The SBA prefers an owner's equity investment of at least 25 percent of the total cost of the project. While no fixed legal requirement exists, the SBA and the lender want proof that the entrepreneur will not abandon the business at the first sign of trouble. The specific amount of an owner's investment can often be negotiated so that a lesser percentage of financing may come from the owner. An SBA guarantee is especially helpful to small businesses that need long-term credit but cannot afford the large equity downpayment, often around 30 percent, required by conventional lenders (CCH 2002).

Pre-qualification Pilot Programs

This program enables the SBA to pre-qualify loan guaranties for business owners before they approach lenders. The SBA claims the program focuses on an applicant's character, credit, experience and reliability rather than her collateral. An SBA-designated nonprofit intermediary, such as a Small Business Development Corporation (SBDC), works with a business owner to review and strengthen the loan application. The review is based on key financial ratios, credit history, business history, and the proposed use of the proceeds.

This pilot program targets several disadvantaged groups, including low and moderate-income persons, the disabled, and businesses from poor rural areas, to name a few. In the recent past, the SBA has piloted Women and Minority "Prequal" Programs. The Pre-qualification Loan Program is available through several SBA district offices, but is not available in all areas.

This program is significant in that it emphasizes technical assistance to entrepreneurs prior to the loan process. Banks should be interested in pre-qualified loan applicants, since much of the SBA paperwork is already completed for them. But, banks will still assess the loan applicant using their own analysis of the loan, the business, and the entrepreneur. Pre-qualification for a guarantee does not assure one of receiving a loan.

Low Documentation Loan (LowDoc)

Currently, the most popular form of financial assistance from the SBA is through the agency's Low Documentation ("LowDoc") Program (CCH 2002). At its essence the LowDoc program is a streamlined version of 7(a). It follows 7(a) policies on interest rates, collateral, and guaranty percentages. Maturity requirements are somewhat different, however. While the maximum period for a fixed asset loan is still 25 years, working capital loans have a five- to ten-year maturity. The repayment period is also determined by the borrower's ability to pay. The SBA encourages small loans under this program by allowing lenders making loans of $50,000 or less with maturity greater than 12 months to retain half of the guarantee fee that is normally paid to the SBA (CCH 2002).

Borrower eligibility also varies somewhat from the requirement of the 7(a) program. For LowDoc eligibility the borrower must be borrowing for the express purpose of starting and growing a business. The size of the business is limited to 100 employees maximum. In addition the borrowing company may not have exceeded $5 million in average annual sales for the three years preceding the loan application. Of course, creditworthiness and character are of concern as well. It should also be noted that LocDoc loans can be for no more than $150,000.

The principal difference between 7(a) and LowDoc loan guarantees, is the attempt to streamline the latter. The program was a response to the ongoing complaints about SBA 7(a), that it is too bureaucratic with excessive paperwork and time for approval. Although the LowDoc program requires less documentation than the SBA previously required, one must still submit certain paperwork. An application for an SBA loan guarantee is submitted through the participating lender and the lender typically uses its ordinary loan application and processing procedures. The lender and applicant together complete the SBA's one-page guaranty application. The borrower completes the front side and the lender completes the back. Then, the lender submits the completed application package to the SBA. For a guarantee on a loan of $50,000 or less, the SBA additionally requires: (1) proof that a conventional lender denied the borrower a loan; (2) a personal financial statement; and a personnel guarantee from anyone owning 20 percent or more of the business. For loan requests for $50,000 to $150,000, the borrower must submit the same documents as for loans under $50,000, plus: (1) copies of the applicant's tax returns for the prior two years; and (2) year-end statements for the last two years (CCH 2002). A decision on the loan is generally provided within thirty-six hours, but not more than one week.

SBAExpress

Formerly known as FA$TRAK, this is a relatively new program that was piloted at selected banks nationwide. In order to qualify for an SBA-

Express loan, a business must meet the SBA's definition of a small business, as measured either by number of employees or average annual sales. As with the LowDoc program, the maximum loan size is $150,000. The maturity caps are the same as for LowDoc as well. Interest rates are consistent with those of the 7(a) program.

The SBA only guarantees Express loans for 50 percent. However, the program minimizes paperwork and permits lenders to use their own forms and processes. Lenders can also use electronic loan processing. The SBA's response time is 36 hours or less. Thus, while the guarantees are not as good, the red tape and wait time surrounding most SBA loan guarantees is greatly reduced. It is hoped that this will act as an incentive to private lenders to become, or remain, active in the medium-risk lending market.

Two programs that are variations on the SBAExpress program are worth noting. They are the SBA Export Express Pilot Loan Program and Community Express. As its name implies, the former focuses on assisting small businesses that face obstacles to getting financing for their export activities. This is a pilot program, and it is anticipated that it will continue through September of 2005.

The Export Express Pilot Program seeks to assist small companies that have exporting potential but lack the financial capital to buy or produce needed goods or services. Loans for up to $150,000 can be used for working capital, real estate purchases, expansion costs, and equipment and inventory purchases. Otherwise, this program works very much like SBA's Express program.

The key distinguishing factor of the Export Express program is the technical assistance it provides to borrowing companies. This takes the form of help with planning, management, and marketing. SBA draws upon a network of its own service provider organizations to deliver this assistance. These include the Service Corps of Retired Executives (SCORE), the Small Business Development Centers (SBDCs), the Export Trade Assistance Partnership, the District Export Council, and the Export Legal Assistance Network. Therefore, much like microenterprise programs, this SBA program attempts to be comprehensive in its business development assistance, offering both access to capital and technical training.

Community Express is also a pilot program. It was developed through a collaborative effort between the SBA and the National Community Reinvestment Coalition (NCRC). The program is designed to provide SBA-Express to businesses located in low-to-moderate-income areas. In a departure from SBAExpress, the maximum loan amount is $250,000. Community Express offers technical assistance to borrowers that is either arranged for, or provided by, the local lending institution. The program is currently limited to certain designated geographic areas and to selected lenders. The purpose of Community Express is, of course, to encourage lending to small businesses that operate in neighborhoods, communities, or regions that are economically disadvantaged. It represents an attempt to target both capital and technical assistance to declining communities.

SBA CAPlines

SBA loan guarantee programs traditionally focused upon the difficulties that small businesses have in obtaining middle-to-long-term financing. To help businesses with the recurring, cyclical, short-term capital shortages that they often face, the SBA broadened and consolidated several of its prior loan guarantee programs into a new program called CAPlines (CCH 2002). Under this program, loan proceeds generally will be advanced against a borrower's existing or anticipated inventory and/or accounts receivable.

CAPlines offers SBA loan guarantees on working capital loans and lines of credit. The repayment schedule of the guaranteed bank loans must be tied to the business's cash cycle, rather than to an arbitrary time schedule. A cash cycle is the period between a business's acquisition of inventory or signing of a service contract and the business's receipt of payment for the sale of the good or service.

CAPlines loan guarantees can be obtained for seasonal needs, specific contracts, building contractor's needs, or for general business purposes such as operating capital, inventory purchasing, and consolidation of short-term debt. The line must be adequately secured by accounts receivable or inventory. The loans can be structured as: (1) a straight line of credit; (2) a revolving line of credit; (3) a fixed line of credit, or (4) a seasonal line. Only one line of credit can be outstanding at any time. A straight line of credit is like a term loan with one- to five-year maturity. A fixed line of credit is short-term with repayment tied to a specific contract or project. A seasonal line is very short-term (as short as thirty days) to provide a business with operating capital to get through a seasonal swing (CCH 2002).

As subprograms of CAPlines, several types of loans may be guaranteed to finance the short-term, cyclical working-capital needs of small businesses. Here, we look at four, asset-based seasonal, contract, and builder's lines of credit

Asset-based Lines of Credit. SBA through CAPlines can guarantee asset-based revolving lines of credit with terms up to five years. Borrowers are allowed to draw and repay as their cash cycle dictates, up to the approved amount of the account, throughout the term of the loan. A borrower cannot simply draw down the line of credit (borrow the maximum amount) and make only interest payments until maturity. Such an arrangement would have to be a term loan.

Asset-based lines of credit were previously available through the SBA's "Greenline" program. Unfortunately, the Greenline program was expensive for banks to administer because of the need to monitor each business's accounts receivable and inventory. Few private lenders had tracking systems that met the SBA's stringent quality standards. Particularly for smaller lines of credit, bank monitoring was not cost-effective.

Now, under the CAPlines program, the SBA divides asset-based lines of credit into two categories: under $200,000, and $200,000 or more. The auditing and cash-management requirements for lines of credit less than $200,000 are relaxed to reduce costs. Banks are also permitted to charge up to 2 percent as a loan-servicing fee. Despite the improvements, the expense of properly administering an SBA-guaranteed line of credit continues to deter most conventional lenders from extending small lines (CCH 2002).

Seasonal Lines of Credit. The CAPlines seasonal lines of credit are SBA guaranteed short-term loans that help small businesses avoid cash crunches attributable to seasonal changes in business volume. The loan proceeds may be used to finance seasonal receivables and inventory. To qualify, a small business must exhibit an established seasonal pattern. The life of the seasonal line of credit loan may not exceed twelve months from the date of the loan's first disbursement. Only one seasonal line of credit loan may be outstanding at any one time and each loan must be followed by a debt-free period of at least one month (CCH 2002).

Contract Lines of Credit. In the past, SBA assisted small businesses with short-term financing of the labor and material costs associated with a specific, assignable contract. The current CAPline program adds a revolving feature. Small construction, manufacturing and service contractors, and subcontractors who provide a specific product or service under a written contract are eligible for this program. Loan proceeds must be used to finance the labor and materials necessary to comply with the terms of the contract. The SBA permits a loan term of up to five years for a contract line of credit. The private lender may require a sub-note demanding earlier repayment. Collateral includes an assignment of contract proceeds. The business might also have to pledge other assets or personal guaranties (CCH 2002).

Builders' Lines of Credit. SBA loan guarantees for short-term loans and lines of credit are available to building contractors to finance the construction or renovation of residential and commercial buildings for sale. Eligible businesses include all construction contractors and homebuilders that meet SBA size and policy standards. The loan maturity may not exceed five years. Loan proceeds must be used for expenses directly associated with acquisition, construction, and/or rehabilitation of the residential or commercial structures.

The bank may require that principal be repaid in a single payment when the project is sold. Interest must be paid at least twice a year. Interest rates are negotiated with the lender but may not exceed SBA's maximum interest rates under its regular guarantee loan program.

Loans must be secured with not less than a second lien on the property to be renovated or constructed. The total amount of the first and second liens cannot exceed 80 percent of the contractor's anticipated selling price (CCH 2002).

Export Working Capital Program (EWCP)

Another SBA loan guaranty program designed to help small businesses that engage in exporting is the Export Working Capital Program (EWCP). The purpose of the EWCP is to make working capital available to small exporting firms in the short term. The loan proceeds may be used for pre-export costs of labor and materials, financing receivables from sales, or standby letters of credit used as performance bonds or payment guarantees to international buyers.

The EWCP is also a very streamlined program, with a one-page application form and a 10-day approval time. The SBA will guarantee loans in the amount of $1,111,111 or less. The guaranteed portion, in this case, runs to a maximum of 90 percent or $1 million. The Export-Import Bank processes loans in excess of the SBA limits. The SBA can increase its exposure to $1.25 million, if the EWCP loan is combined with an international trade loan.

The guaranteed bank loans can be structured as revolving lines of credit or term loans, or be tied to a specific contract or cash cycle. EWCP loans that involve single transactions are limited to a maximum term of eighteen months. Loans for multiple transactions have a maturity of twelve months. These can be renewed twice, permitting a maximum period of three years.

While the SBA does not dictate interest rates for EWCP loans, it does monitor them to ensure reasonableness. Another unique aspect of EWCP loan guarantees is that each business that applies must submit a cash flow projection as a way of substantiating the need for the loan and the ability to repay it. Once the loan is made, the borrower must continue to provide regular progress reports.

The EWCP loan guarantees are targeted at helping small businesses to be more active exporters in the global economy. As with all SBA programs, the borrowers must be companies that would not otherwise have been able to obtain debt capital from private lending sources.

While exporting may offer tremendous market potential for certain small companies, additional research and preparation expenses are necessary for developing and implementing an international business plan. Additional costs may include multinational legal compliances such as labeling, packaging, product safety, and liability laws; tailored marketing for different countries and languages; transportation costs for product delivery and personnel travel; and export licenses.

During its short life, EWCP has been used almost exclusively for credit of one year or less, with revolving lines accounting for about two-thirds of loan guarantees under the program. Borrowers have generally been either manufacturers or wholesalers (CCH 2002).

These export program guarantees replace the SBA's prior program, the Export Working Lines of Credit Program that offered short-term, revolving lines of credit. The program is the product of collaboration between the SBA and the Export-Import Bank. It is scheduled to continue until September 2005 (CCH 2002).

International Trade Loan (ITL)

This program provides short- and long-term financing to small businesses that are engaged or preparing to engage in exporting, as well as businesses adversely affected by import competition. The SBA can guarantee up to $1.25 million for a combination of fixed-asset financing and working capital. From this limit one must subtract the amount of any other SBA guarantees outstanding to the borrower. Only $750,000 may be for working capital needs.

In addition to meeting the general eligibility criteria for a SBA loan guarantee, a small business applicant for the International Trade Loan Program must establish either of the following:

- The loan proceeds will significantly expand existing export markets or develop new export markets. (The applicant must submit a business plan including sufficient information to support the likelihood of expanded export sales.)

- The applicant is adversely affected by import competition. Injury attributable to increased competition with foreign firms must be demonstrated. A narrative explanation and financial statements must show that directly competitive imported products have contributed significantly to a decline in the firm's competitive position. Damage can be demonstrated through factors such as sales or production declines, underutilized capacity, decreased profitability, or potential loss of production employees.

The working capital portion of the loan must be made according to the provisions of the Export Working Capital Program (EWCP).

The loan proceeds may be used for: (1) working capital; (2) purchasing, building, renovating, expanding or improving facilities or equipment: and (3) making other improvements that will be used within the United States for producing goods or services. Proceeds may not be used for debt repayment.

The lender must take a first lien on the items financed under this section, and only collateral located in the United States may be pledged. Additional supportive collateral may be required, including personal guaranties and subordinate liens on items that are not financed by loan proceeds.

Maturities of loans for facilities or equipment may extend to the twenty-five-year maximum applicable to most SBA loan guarantee programs. The working capital portion of loans has a three-year maturity. Lenders may charge 2.25 or 2.75 percentage points above the prime rate, depending on the maturity of the loan. The interest rate on EWCP loans is not regulated.

This program has not been used by small businesses as much as the Export Working Capital Program. The Section 7(a) loan guarantee program is probably being used in lieu of ITL for capital needs under $1 million.

Evaluation of the SBA Loan Guarantee Programs

Lender Perspective

From the point of view of the bank or other recognized lending institution, the various SBA loan guarantee programs afford greatly reduced risk. With 75 to 85 percent of the loan typically guaranteed, bankers need much less collateral to feel that the risk is fully covered. Also, some commercial lenders prefer an SBA-guaranteed small business loan because they have a readily available secondary market in which to sell the guaranteed portion of the loan. In addition, the guaranteed portion of the loan does not count against the federally mandated reserve funds that banks must maintain as protection against loan losses (CCH 2002). Some nonbank SBA-certified lenders such as BIDCOs (see section on BIDCOs in this chapter), might not make many SBA guaranteed loans, but they add a few 7(a) loans to their portfolio. They see the low risk associated with the guaranteed portion of the loan as adding stability to their medium-risk portfolio (Sandstedt 2002).

Banks, however, are not often anxious to get involved with SBA programs. They sometimes feel that the paperwork is not worth the benefit. Some studies have indicated that a relatively small percentage of banks make a majority of SBA loans. In 1985 about 19 percent of the participating banks made 70 percent of the SBA loans, and the banking industry has become more concentrated since (Hayes 1993). After the bank approves a loan, it must work with the borrower to apply for the SBA guarantee. Average time for completing a successful 7(a) loan guarantee package is approximately 25 hours.

Borrower Perspective

From the borrower's perspective, the SBA 7(a) program is often seen as life-saving access to needed capital. A study by PriceWaterhouse reports that businesses that receive SBA loan guarantees exhibit higher growth than comparable businesses. However, the program has not been without its frustrations for businesses. While most entrepreneurs can complete a LowDoc application, with the assistance of the private lender, a Section 7(a) loan guarantee application is considerably more complicated. The price range for professional assistance in completing their loan application is approximately $1,200–$5,000 (CCH 2002).

Turnaround time on these applications can range from several weeks to months. Some refer to the main 7(a) program as "HiDoc." Since the federal taxpayer is shouldering a high percentage of the risk with a federal loan guarantee program, the SBA must review the loan with the same due diligence as if it were making the loan. This means that the applicant must go through the entire loan application process with two agents, the bank and the SBA, but with different forms and looking for slightly different information. Never-ending complaints about this process help explain why SBA has tried so many different forms of the program over the years, including the low-documentation and express forms of the program and the pre-qualification schemes.

The LowDoc program has been successful and popular, permitting nearly 90 percent of applicants to obtain financing. Bureaucratic delays caused by protracted loan approval procedures have been reduced. The processing time for a LowDoc application is usually less than one week. Yet, as one borrower put it," LowDoc isn't no doc." One must still go through the lender's loan evaluation process and submit to the SBA financials, tax forms, pro formas, certifications, and personal guarantees. The express program offers greater speed and less process, but the guarantee for the bank is only 50 percent of the bank loan. Most of the other specialized guarantee programs follow 7(a) procedures.

Entrepreneurs do not have time to become knowledgeable about all relevant loan guarantee programs. Businesses sometimes have trouble finding the right program niche and then finding a bank willing to participate in that specialized program.

Community Perspective

Basic SBA loan guarantees have been with us for nearly half a century. Given the dearth of other mechanisms to promote small business-oriented midrisk debt capital, the benefit to the nation and local community economies has been great. Currently, these programs operate at relatively low cost as the SBA makes a particular effort to offset the expense of their loan guarantee programs to taxpayers by charging participating lenders guaranty and servicing fees.

Recent SBA program innovations improve the way loan guarantees target business and community needs and reduce the bureaucratic red tape that encumbers them. The Export Express, EWCP, and Community Express programs are prime examples. The first two are focused on increasing the availability of debt capital to small businesses that export. In this way, the SBA is encouraging and supporting these companies in participating in the global economy. It is helping them meet some of the challenges presented by a world economy that were discussed in Chapter 1. The Community Express program targets low- and moderate-income communities and regions. It seeks to overcome the obstacles to obtaining working capital that many entrepreneurs face in inner-city neighborhoods and rural regions. It assists low- and moderate-income people in building a business, which, in turn, allows them to build wealth. It does so not merely by generating income but by creating assets as well. Assets can be transferred intergenerationally, thereby helping to sustain wealth (Oliver and Shapiro 1995). Experiments with pre-qualification programs for minorities and women could have similar community benefits.

All three of these programs, along with SBA LowDoc, try to streamline the loan guarantee process. This is attractive to both private lenders and borrowing companies. One more barrier to participation by lending institutions is removed, and borrowers do not have to wait for extended periods of time to learn whether or not they will receive a loan. By speeding access to money for fixed assets and working capital, the SBA permits small businesses to react more quickly to market opportunities, thereby making them more competitive in global markets.

On a more basic level, the federal government, through the SBA, is intervening in debt capital markets to perfect those markets by filling the gap in capital provision that exists between direct government lending to higher-risk businesses and conventional private lending. Without this intervention, almost bankable (medium-risk) firms would have had very few options over the last 50 years for capital infusions. Thus, this is an appropriate government intervention in the free market. It addresses an equity issue by putting medium-risk small businesses on a more equal footing with others with regard to capital access. In the bargain, it enhances the chances for success for a wider range of entrepreneurs, which facilitates community economic development.

Despite these advantages, SBA loan guarantee programs have had their limitations and have been subject to criticism. SBA has been criticized at times for being too stingy. At other times they have been criticized for inducing businesses to borrow more than was appropriate. At one point some said SBA had too high a loan failure rate, particularly among minority programs with less stringent criteria. Some banks and businesses continue to feel the program is somewhat cumbersome, even under the newer "Low Doc" rules.

Because of these criticisms, the SBA has formulated a plethora of optional loan guarantee programs with various rules for different business situations. The desire is to keep banks and businesses interested in participating while, at the same time, managing the variable risk associated with differential environments. In other words, writing specific rules for each situation is an attempt to artificially balance risks with rewards for all stakeholders in a variety of cases. The SBA finds itself continuously experimenting with guarantee levels, collateral requirements, interest caps, loan sizes, and maturities in an attempt to have a program available for every environment. Sometimes, the program they devise gets few takers, or goes into disuse. Current examples might include the International Loan Program and the CAPlines asset-based revolving loans.

In defense of the SBA, finding the right balance between ease of use and due diligence is not easy, partly because it is a moving target. A loan guarantee program with a particular guarantee percent, interest, term, collateral, and use of proceeds, might be good for one part of the business cycle but not another. A program, for example, that provides a 75 percent guarantee, that allows banks to charge 2.75 percent over prime, is backed by receivables and must be paid back before the next seasonal cycle, might be acceptable to all parties in one economic environment, but not in another. All of this means that bank attorneys, loan officers, entrepreneurs, and small business service providers must spend much time learning a large number of regulations and staying on top of program changes.

The SBA's recent efforts to meet business needs are commendable and have exhibited evidence of some success. They help to perfect capital markets by diversifying intermediary processes. Yet, many of the difficulties the program has faced over the years are because the loan guarantee concept, as utilized by the SBA, does not always respond well to market forces. Loan guarantee programs share risk, but they do not distribute risk in a manner that causes all actors, including competing banks and businesses, to respond. Sometimes, the incentives and the potential rewards that induce various stakeholders to participate have little relationship to the costs or risks stakeholders face. Participants who share greater risk do not necessarily receive commensurately greater rewards. This is because much of the risk/reward distribution process is set by law (maximum interest rates, maturities, fees, etc.) rather than allowed to respond to market situations.

Some aspects of the program do attempt to create a natural balance between risks and rewards. For example, banks are rewarded with higher maximum interest rates if they make longer maturity loans. Yet, in some ways, the incentives associated with the loan guarantee process work contrary to market forces. Banks are induced to seek the highest level of guarantee possible to minimize risk. But, this strategy adds little to their costs and does not decrease potential rewards. Business incentives are also often counterintuitive. On the one hand, to be eligible, businesses have to be so risky that they are unable to receive conventional loans from lending institutions. On the other hand, the businesses must be so sound and safe that they exhibit little chance of failure. They must prove this soundness with collateral, personal guarantees, multi-year business projections, and positive cash flow pro formas. They must also grow and create jobs. If a business can fit into this theoretically narrow niche it can receive a significant subsidy from the government in the form of a low-cost loan guarantee. On the other hand the taxpayer continues to be the primary at-risk stakeholder, requiring the SBA to be even more diligent than banks in loan analysis. This fact produces high governmental administrative costs. Much of the loan decision is in the lap of the SBA loan officer. S/he must make the decision based purely on the paper put on the desk, with little guidance from the marketplace. This causes the program to be slow and bureaucratic and leaves SBA open to constant criticism. The capital access program described in the next section better addresses many of these issues.

Furthermore, access to capital, alone, does not ensure business success. Business failure postmortems are full of stories about entrepreneurs who received capital only to squander it because they did not know how to use it effectively. The SBA has tried to address this in its more recent full programs and pilot programs by offering technical assistance in conjunction with their pre-qualification mechanism and other loan guarantee programs. This is a step in the right direction; however, determination of what technical assistance is required is being left, in effect, to the entrepreneur. As Lichtenstein and Lyons (1996) have pointed out, one of the major obstacles to entrepreneurial success is a lack of self-awareness on the part of the entrepreneur as to what his or her needs are. Without a thorough assessment of skill-building needs, involving both the service provider and the entrepreneur, no one really knows what the latter needs in order to be successful.

Along similar lines, it is not always made clear to the entrepreneur where mezzanine capital fits into the larger scheme of capital provision. While the SBA may be well aware of where their loan guarantees fit, their ultimate clients may have misperceptions about why they are or are not receiving a loan. Furthermore, they may see the loan as a one-time capital infusion. This can create problems down the road, as borrowers find that the money was adequate for their immediate needs but that it took their businesses to a higher level of evolution that required still more capital. Entrepreneurs who do not understand this phenomenon tend to blame the capital provider for setting them up to fail by loaning them too little. They need to understand that the SBA-backed loan they receive is a bridge across the gap to bankability and that it is merely a single step along the path to their own transformation as an entrepreneur and that of their business.

LOAN INSURANCE POOLING: THE CAPITAL ACCESS PROGRAM

The Loan Insurance Pool Concept

One governmental approach to promoting medium-risk/reward financing for small businesses is loan insurance. Governmental loan insurance programs are even less invasive and direct than loan guarantees. Like most insurance policies, loan insurance spreads risk among many clients, thus reducing the cost to each, while providing some protection for all. It works by establishing a fund- or loan-loss reserve pool. The pool becomes an insurance program that can be used to cover a bank's loses resulting from a non-performing loan. Theoretically, with this backing, lenders are willing to lend to higher-risk customers than they otherwise would. The pool is funded through fees or non-refundable deposits provided by participating higher risk borrowers.

Unlike a loan guarantee, the pool does not just cover the loan in question. The pool insures a portfolio of participating loans for which similar deposits have been made into the same pool. For the concept to work, the fee level for the purchase of insurance must be in balance with the level of risk created by the loans. If the balance were to be attained, the inflow of fees into the pool would equal or exceed the outflow caused by bad loans. A slight excess inflow would allow the pool to build up over time.

While this has been a workable concept for decades, neither banks nor other lenders have pursued it vigorously on their own. They have either felt that an adequate pool would be too difficult to build, or that the fees necessary to justify the risk would be beyond what businesses would pay. Bank regulators do not always encourage the use of the concept and often do not assign much value to insurance protection (Hamlin 1998). They point out that, while a loan guarantee is a legally binding commitment to stand behind some designated percent of a loan, loan insurance commitments are only as strong as the insurance pool. Hypothetically, in a severe recession, a greater-than-expected number of participating loans could become non-performing and drain the pool of its value. At that point, all other participating loans would have no backing. Losses would then reduce the net worth of the lender.

For government to provide direct or subsidized loans or even to guarantee loans for higher-risk businesses has inherent problems. The first problem is the potential cost to taxpayers if loans are not repaid. A second problem is that governments are political bodies that might not have sufficient financial objectivity for proper "due diligence." Governments often do not have the expertise to assess (1) the potential of the business, (2) whether the terms of the loan are appropriate for the risk, and (3) whether terms and conditions are in line with the prevailing market. If any of these issues are not well addressed, then government intervention might distort money markets rather than perfect them. Direct loan programs may make higher risk borrowing too easy, for example. They might upset the risk/reward balance, inducing borrowers and lenders to take too much risk by going too deeply into debt. This imbalance often hurts the small business more than it helps, and could create unfair competition for unsubsidized businesses. These criticisms have occasionally been directed at U.S. SBA programs as discussed in the previous section.

As in all good public/private partnerships, market forces should be utilized to the extent possible. Government can lubricate the financial intermediary process for medium-risk situations by carefully sharing some of the risk and fomenting institutions that facilitate that process. This should be done in such a way that requires all actors to carry a substantial portion of the risk so that they will act with appropriate care.

Governments interested in promoting capital flows to middle-risk businesses can use loan insurance pools. Loan insurance utilizes market forces, but history tells us that, in order for loan insurance pools to exist, government must be involved. So, how should government carefully intervene in the capital markets to accomplish the public goal of midrisk small business finance using loan insurance? At the very least, that involvement must strongly and formally sanction the concept of loan insurance and create appropriate legal and organizational structures. Government might also share some of the risk as a way of tipping the scales and inducing all other parties to become involved. Risk sharing might take a variety of forms, including governmental deposits in the loan insurance pools. Programs to do these things are called Capital Access Programs (CAP), and have sprung up around the country.

The Capital Access Program to Promote Loan Insurance Pooling: History and Purpose

"Capital Access Program" (CAP) was a name given to a government-sponsored loan insurance pool concept started in Michigan in 1986. It was one of a set of business tools implemented as a part of the Michigan Strategic fund at a time when the Great Lakes states were experiencing severe economic restructuring. Use of the concept has now spread to more than twenty states and two cities. Because of its age, the Michigan program has been the largest, both in loans and dollars. At the end of 1999 the Michigan CAP accounted for over one-third of all CAP loans granted in the nation. New states continue to begin the programs. Texas and Illinois enacted CAPs and began operating their programs in 1997 (U.S. Treasury1998). Florida, Louisiana, and Maryland began in 1999 and 2000, and Hawaii plans to begin soon (U.S. Treasury 2001).

The Capital Access Program of Michigan was, from the beginning, an attempt to address intermediate-risk capital needs by perfecting capital markets with minimal governmental intervention. The program has always been one of the most flexible, with the least restrictions on bank behavior. Rightly or wrongly, many other states have injected additional rules, restrictions, or targeting incentives over time.

Three years ago, the Michigan CAP was made a part of the Michigan Economic Development Corporation (MEDC), a relatively new quasi-public state corporation charged with the state's economic development. Despite positive independent analysis of the impacts of Michigan's CAP, the MEDC decided it had different priorities. MEDC recently began the phase-out of the program, making the nation's pioneer program one of the first state CAPs to be phased-out (Hamlin 2002).

How the Capital Access Program Works

Programs all over the United States have similar characteristics. Some of these common mechanics are described below.

Bank Participation. To begin with, banks must agree to participate in the program. If a bank decides to participate, a special loan loss reserve fund is set up to cover future losses from a portfolio of participating loans. The fund may be owned officially by the state but earmarked in that bank's name and deposited in the bank making the loans. Effectively, banks control the pool within the rules of the program. The bank may withdraw funds from the reserve pool only to cover losses on loans made under the program. As described below, payments are made to the pool each time a loan is made under the program. If the bank ever terminates its participation in the program, the state may confiscate the pool. If two banks merge, their pools may be combined (Hamlin 1998).

Businesses Contact the Bank. In seeking the loan, the business owner goes directly to a bank. If the bank finds too many risk factors for the loan requested, the banker might suggest CAP. In that case the bank would offer a loan with conventional terms and conditions, but with the additional requirement that the business make a nonrefundable deposit to the loan loss reserve pool. The contribution is equal to 1.5 percent to 3.5 percent of the loan amount. The exact percentage is the discretion of the bank within the limits allowed by a particular state's program. In fact, all other terms and conditions of the loan are negotiable between the business and borrowers to the same degree that they are with any loan (Michigan Jobs Commission 1996).

Contribution to the Reserve Account. If everyone agrees to the terms, the bank enrolls the loan in the program by faxing a one- or two-page form to the state government within a set number of days of the loan closing.

The governmental agency does *not* complete a financial review of or approve the loan. The form provides the particulars and certifies that the loan meets program eligibility requirements. The bank then matches the business's deposit in the loan loss fund, and the governmental agency matches the combined business-bank contribution. In practice, the bank may pass most of its portion of the premium on to the borrower by financing the premium in the loan proceeds (Michigan Jobs Commission 1996).

States have varying policies with regard to how much they require banks, borrowers, and the state to contribute to the reserve fund. States typically match private contributions dollar-for-dollar, with many states increasing their matching ratio for target groups or areas. All in all, state contributions to the reserve funds typically range from 3 percent to 7 percent of the loan amount, implying public leverage of private funding in a range from 33:1 to 14:1. Nationwide, based on information from eleven states, the state match averages 5 percent of the loan (U.S. Treasury 1998). The pool then acts as last-resort backing for the loan in question, and for all other loans that participate in the program through the same bank.

A few states provide a start-up credit line to give banks, in effect, an advance on future CAP premiums. This helps a bank in the event it experiences an early CAP loss before the reserve fund has built up enough to absorb the full loss. A bank would then repay the credit line from future CAP premiums. Vermont and Pennsylvania provide an initial $50,000 line of credit to their participating banks (U.S. Treasury 1998).

Other programs address this issue by increasing the public matching ratio for banks' initial loans. For example, Michigan provided a two-for-one match for a bank's initial $2 million in loans and then reduced the match to one-to-one. At the same time, many CAPs do not use start-up incentives at all (U.S. Treasury 1998). Some states promote lending to targeted groups or areas, such as Enterprise Zones, by sharing more of the risk for loans in those areas (U.S. Treasury 1998). They do this by enhancing the state match.

Nonperforming Loans/Recovery. If any loan in the portfolio stops performing, the bank must go through the normal recovery process, and pursue all remedies available to it. If the bank ultimately loses money on the loan, it has the right to charge the loss against the pool. Some states allow the bank to charge losses off against the pool as soon as the loan is declared in default and then reimburse the pool if some recovery is accomplished.

The collection and claims process is designed to work in a routine, non-bureaucratic way. The bank uses its normal method for determining when and how much to charge off on a loan. If the bank plans to charge losses off against the CAP pool, the bank files a one-page claim form with the state, with payment to be handled in a prompt and routine fashion (Michigan Jobs Commission 1996).

Building Up the Pool. The program has a snowballing effect. If the bank operates prudently, the pool builds up over time. When a loan is paid off, the contribution from that loan stays in the reserve. This increases protection against losses and provides the bank with greater and greater cover for these riskier loans. "So banks have an incentive to keep adding loans to the program, and to make prudently riskier loans" (Osborne and Plasterik 1997).

The earmarked reserve enables a bank to be more aggressive in making loans and expanding its markets. However, if a bank's loss rate were to exceed the coverage provided by the reserve, the bank's net worth would be at risk for the excess losses. Thus, a built-in incentive causes banks to be prudent (Michigan Jobs Commission 1996).

Nevertheless, since the reserve would enable a bank to withstand a substantially higher loss rate than it could tolerate under its conventional loan portfolio, the program enables a bank to prudently make "almost bankable loans." For example, these loans might be loans to companies with good management and good direction, but for one reason or another are not eligible for conventional bank loans. They might lack adequate collateral, have insufficient track record, or exhibit inadequate net worth to qualify for a conventional loan (Michigan Jobs Commission 1996).

Conceptually, the pool builds up in layers with the government's contribution at the bottom, the bank's contribution in the middle and the contributions from businesses on top. This means that if the pool is ever called on to cover a bad loan, all previous business contributions to the pool are first to be used. Government contributions to the pool are last to be used.

Flexibility/Minimal Government Involvement. Because the program is structured to provide a built-in incentive for the bank to be prudent, the governmental agency has no need to review the bank's decision on the loan. This is very different from the situation for SBA guaranty programs. Under CAP, the reserve is there for the bank to protect and use. Enrolling loans under the program is thus designed to work as essentially an automatic process, with no processing delays and little paperwork (Michigan Jobs Commission 1996). Research verifies these claims (Hamlin 1998).

Flexibility is a key characteristic of the program. It is up to the bank to determine how it wants to use the program. The bank sets its own criteria for determining what types of loans to make, and deciding interest rates, fees, terms of maturity, collateral requirements, and other conditions.

Thus, the market is allowed to work, and intelligent private-sector decision making is facilitated. Loans can be short-term or long-term, fixed or variable rate, secured or unsecured, amortizing or ballooned, term or line of credit (Michigan Jobs Commission 1996). There is no need for a variety of specialized programs with different rules to fit different situations.

The program's flexibility enables a bank to work with a borrower after the loan is closed. The bank may, for example, recast the loan as often as appropriate. It can extend the term of the loan, amend covenants, release collateral, or work with the borrower in a variety of ways normal to most loans. These adjustments may be carried out without obtaining approval from the state, or, in most cases even reporting the changes (Michigan Jobs Commission 1996).

When filing a loan for enrollment under the program, the bank has the option of covering less than the full amount of the loan. Borrower and bank premiums would then be based on this smaller amount. For example, if a bank makes a $200,000 loan, but is convinced that the maximum loss on the loan would be $90,000, the bank could specify to include only $90,000 of the loan in CAP. In such an event, the funds in the reserve pool would be used to cover the first $90,000 in principal loss on the loan, plus accrued interest, plus documented out-of-pocket expenses (Michigan Jobs Commission 1996).

The bank also has the flexibility to refinance the loan, and may add funds. If the total amount of the refinanced loan does not exceed the previously covered amount, no new premium payments need to be made into the reserve fund. The refinancing does not typically need to be reported to the state (Michigan Jobs Commission 1996).

As an example, assume that a $100,000 loan covered under the program has been paid down to $30,000. Then, it is refinanced back up to $100,000. In that case no new premium payments are owed. However, if the loan were instead refinanced up to $150,000, premium payments might be owed only on the incremental $50,000 above the original $100,000. The additional premium would only be necessary if the bank and borrower wanted the additional $50,000 to participate in the program (Michigan Jobs Commission 1996).

Lines of Credit. Lines of credit are treated with similar flexibility. The bank determines a maximum drawn-down amount in its usual way. Any portion of that draw-down limit may then be enrolled in the program and charged a CAP fee. If the business fails, the amount enrolled in CAP is the limit of what draw can be insured by the program. Once having established a line of credit, the bank and business can then renew it each year.

The line stays covered under the program without new payments into the pool being required unless the covered amount under the program is to be increased (Michigan Jobs Commission 1996). This flexibility contrasts dramatically with the multifaceted rules governing the mélange of SBA line-of-credit guarantee programs and subprograms.

Eligibility. In most states, all small businesses are eligible (U.S. Treasury 2001). The fundamental thrust of the program is to make eligibility as broad as possible so as to maximize the effect on the state or local economy and avoid second-guessing market decisions. The borrower may be a corporation, partnership, joint venture, or sole proprietor. Some states even allow cooperatives or nonprofits (Michigan Jobs Commission 1996). Some states impose restrictions. Common ones are to make an industry ineligible, restrict loan size or business size, or restrict the use of proceeds.

With respect to eligible industries, housing investment is often excluded, but motel and hotel debt may be eligible. Passive real-estate ownership is often excluded, but some states allow real-estate mortgages for active business property used by the borrowing small business concern to be included. Developers and contractors may also receive CAP participating loans in some cases (U.S. Treasury1998).

Some states impose restrictions on the loan size. For example, in one state, the maximum loan size is capped at $150,000. This limits the availability of CAP lending for small businesses that require larger loans, and it potentially discourages bank participation. It does not appear that loan size and loan default rates are correlated (U.S. Treasury1998).

Other states restrict the size of the borrowing business (U.S. Treasury, 1998) to ensure that the assistance goes to small businesses. Michigan placed no limits on the borrower size or loan sizes (Hamlin 1998). The state claimed that the structure of the program tended to focus the program on assisting small and medium-sized companies. Michigan did limit the amount it would pay into any bank's loan loss reserve pool in support of participating loans for any one borrower. It would contribute no more than $150,000 over a three-year period without special permission from the state. Research indicates that even though Michigan imposed no business size restrictions, nearly all of the participating loans were to small businesses.

Refinancing of existing debt is another eligibility issue in many states. Generally, as in other economic development programs, refinancing use is limited since government wants to generate new investment that will create new jobs. Yet, refinancing flexibility can often make the deal. Usually, if a package adds new money to a refinanced loan, at least the new money can participate in the program (U.S. Treasury1998).

Another eligibility issue is whether the business must prove that it cannot obtain a loan in another way. This requirement is added to many government programs to ensure that the business needs the program and that the program is not crowding out activities that the private sector could handle conventionally. Under the SBA 7(a), for example, loan guarantee borrowers must prove that they cannot receive conventional financing under reasonable terms. CAP programs generally allow the marketplace to handle this issue. Because of the payments that need to be made into the reserve, a loan made under CAP is likely to be more expensive to the borrower than a conventional bank loan. Thus, borrowers who can obtain conventional bank financing to meet their needs would logically be better off with conventional terms. Theoretically, competition within the banking industry will steer such borrowers to conventional financing. However, this assumes that borrowers are fully informed, rational, and have flexibility in choice of lender (Berger and Undel 1995).

In reality, premium payments into the reserve are one-time, up-front payments, the costs of which can be amortized. Thus, the longer the financing stays on the books, the smaller the increase in the borrower's effective interest rate caused by CAP fees. Moreover, financing under the CAP is likely to be less expensive than alternative non-bank sources (Michigan Jobs Commission 1996).

Analysis and Evaluation of the Program

The following information for this analysis is available from two studies. They are a periodic nationwide survey conducted by the U.S. Treasury Department in 1997 and 2000, and an in-depth analysis of the Michigan CAP, the largest program in the country, conducted by the Institute for Public Policy and Social Research at Michigan State University. The national data is a result of a fax questionnaire from the Community Development Financial Institutions Program Office of the U.S. Department of Treasury to state and city program operators. The information collected included fundamental tracking statistics and program legal information. Nearly identical questions were asked each year and response rates were nearly 100 percent. Analysis consisted of basic statistical summaries and compilation of non-quantitative responses.

The Michigan program has been operating for nearly fifteen years. Because it was the oldest and largest CAP in the nation, an in-depth analysis of that program was undertaken in 1998 which included comprehensive interviews and analyses of 350 participating businesses, six participating banks, and economic development professions. Truly objective, independent analyses of an economic development program is rare, and the Michigan program is particularly interesting for at least three reasons. First, the Michigan program, at the time of the study amounted to over one-third of national CAP loan volume. Second, it was one of the most flexible, relying heavily on market forces. Third, the program is now being phased out for reasons unrelated to the study, making an independent assessment more timely. For these reasons, Michigan data is used extensively in this section.

The ultimate question the study addressed was whether the program was promoting the growth and diversity of the state's economy and therefore generating jobs, tax revenues, and greater economic stability for the state. In the process, a great deal of other information was found. Some of the information includes an estimation of the appropriateness of the loans, the degree to which the program has created jobs, the tax revenues generated by the new economic activity, and the economic diversity produced. These are discussed below.

Number and Size of Loans, Businesses. Total CAP lending nationwide was $1.56 billion as of mid-2000 as a result of about 25,725 loans. CAP lending has been especially pronounced in three states: Michigan, California, and Massachusetts had been responsible for nearly 70 percent of cumulative volume. Michigan, which has been the largest program in the country by a significant margin, was responsible for 36 percent of all CAP lending (U.S. Treasury1998). The nationwide average size of a CAP loan is $60,625. This figure has been gradually increasing over time and varies considerably across states. California produces the largest average loan, at $155,000, and Vermont produces the smallest, at $7,500 (U.S. Treasury 2001).

National data on the size of businesses receiving CAP loans is not available. Some programs have size restrictions and some do not. The Michigan study divided businesses into two sample groups called "larger businesses" and "smaller businesses." Michigan data show that 14 percent of CAP borrowers were in the larger group that had sales equal to or greater than $1,000,000 and 86 percent were the smaller businesses with sales less than $1,000,000. Michigan has had no loan or business-size restrictions or special targeting of loans to small businesses. Yet, the Michigan program clearly worked to the benefit of small businesses (Hamlin 1998).

No national data exists for the age of businesses. Based on the Michigan study results, for businesses with average annual sales greater than or equal to $1 million, the mean business age at the time of the CAP loan was fourteen years. Nearly every business in the sample was a mature organization that had survived at least one recession. Among the firms with under $1 million in sales, the average age of a business at the time of a CAP loan was six years. Thirty-one percent of these loans in Michigan were to start-up businesses. If start-ups are deleted from the average-age calculation, the average of the remaining smaller-business sample was about nine years. Again, the majority were mature businesses (Hamlin 1998).

Lending by Industrial Sector. Six states provided industry-specific loan information to the U.S. Treasury survey, and the data show that CAP loans are able to cover a broad spectrum of business types. CAP loans in these states have been made most often to construction, manufacturing, retail, and service businesses, while also reaching wholesale and transportation firms with significant frequency. The available data also indicate that CAP lending is able to tailor itself to the needs of particular states. For example, for five of the six states reporting, agribusiness loans represented only 1 to 3 percent of the state total, but in Arkansas agribusiness lending comprises 50 percent of all CAP loans (U.S. Treasury 1998).

Some states only lend to a limited set of industries. Most notably, public CAP funds in California are generated through environmental bond issues, and regulations require that these dollars be used to support businesses that affect the environment. California's program administrators estimate that 40 to 50 percent of possible borrowers are excluded by this limitation (U.S. Treasury 1998). Two states target particular industries for extra state match, but the available data are insufficient to assess the impact of this targeting.

The Michigan study confirmed the broad industrial coverage of the program found in the national survey. The percent of businesses of each major type in Michigan, based on SIC codes, is shown in Table 4.1.

Table 4.1
Percentages of Businesses Receiving CAP Loans in Michigan, by SIC Code

Business Type	SIC Code	Larger Firms (sales ≥ $1 M)	Smaller Firms (sales < $1 M)
Agriculture	0	2%	1%
Mining & Construction	1	12	5
Manufacturing	2 & 3	25	14
Transportation	4	8	4
Wholesale Transportation	5	10	7
Retail	5	21	33
Finance, Ins. & Real Estate	6	2	1
Service	7 & 8	18	32
Nonprofit	-	1	2

Source: Hamlin, Roger E. 1998. *The Capital Access Program: An Evaluation of Economic Benefit.* Lansing, MI: The Michigan Jobs Commission.

Knowing the industry of a business and its product or service is important to assess risk. Some types of businesses are considered inherently
risky by banks and are almost always put into CAP. One such category is
small retail establishments, particularly those that may face sudden competition from a major chain store or department stores such as Walmart. As
can be seen from the table above, a high percentage of the smaller businesses participating in CAP are retail establishments.

Another example of what business lenders consider to be high risk is
construction contractors. Lenders complain that contractors have "com-
pletion of work" problems such as bonds, liens, and other risks associated
with being paid for a construction project. As a result they are nearly
always put into CAP. It is notable that both the national survey and Michigan study found that CAPs seem to be reaching businesses, such as building contractors and wholesale trade companies, that are typically not well
reached by any other credit enhancement programs.

All interviewed banks said that restaurants are inherently risky because
of a perpetual oversupply. Adding to the list are (1) businesses especially
vulnerable to national business cycles, (2) businesses with only one major
customer, (3) nonprofit corporations, and (4) high-liability businesses such
as child care and foster care. The Michigan study found that these are all
candidates for CAP participation no matter how strong their current balance sheet may be.

Loan Losses and Reserve Funds. Through the end of June 2000, 691
banks were enrolled in CAPs nationwide and 394 were actively originat-
ing CAP loans. Many of these banks have large branch networks. The
numbers of enrolled banks declined slightly from 1997. Active banks grew
at a 13.5 percent rate over the same period (U.S. Treasury 2001).

Through the end of June 2000, cumulative CAP loan losses nationwide
totaled approximately $58.5 million, or 3.8 percent of all loan volume
extended (U.S. Treasury 2001). The Michigan study confirmed these
results. This loss rate approximates a normal loss rate for conventional
lending. The Michigan study found that smaller participating firms were
more likely to have nonperforming loans (Hamlin 1998). Both the Michigan and national data exhibit that the claim rate, as a percentage of total
annual loans, has been declining for many years, as shown in Figure 4.1.

After subtracting loan losses, banks nationwide still held approximately
$64 million in their CAP reserve funds at the end of June 2000, equal to 4.1
percent of the total loan volume extended. Michigan's total reserves at the end
of 1997 represented one-fifth of the national level at that time (Hamlin 1999).
CAP reserves as a percentage of outstanding loans would be much higher
since much of the cumulative loan volume ($1.5 billion) has been repaid.

Figure 4.1
Number of Loans Making Claims on Pools in Michigan As a Percentage of Total Loans by Year

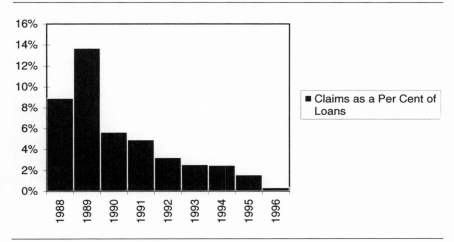

Source: Hamlin, Roger E. 1998. *The Capital Access Program: An Evaluation of Economic Benefit.* Lansing, MI: The Michigan Jobs Commission.

The data suggest that current reserves are adequate to meet future losses, absent unforeseen circumstances. Many CAP loans are for short maturates. Since remaining reserves are 1.1 times as large as historical losses, and most programs are more than a few years old with a substantial loan volume having been repaid, coverage available on outstanding loans appears sufficient (U.S. Treasury 2001). Many new banks have joined CAPs, and banks made a record quantity of new loans. Presumably, those banks believe themselves to be adequately covered. Moreover, some banks with CAP experience in one state are expanding CAP lending to other states (U.S. Treasury 1998).

Effect of State Leverage. One might expect to see a relationship between the size of a state's contribution to its reserve funds and the resulting level of CAP lending. New Hampshire's data support this theory: The public contribution to pools per loan is the second largest in the country, and New Hampshire has the largest level of lending in the nation per-capita. Yet, across the nation, only a weak correlation exists between public contributions and the size of a capital access program. The lack of strong correlation suggests that state contributions are only one factor in determining the relative magnitude of state programs (U.S. Treasury 1998).

Table 4.2
Use of Proceeds: Percent of Michigan Interviewees by Size of Business

business size category- -->	Larger (sales ≥ $1 M)	Smaller (sales < $1 M)
Purpose / Use of Proceeds		
Bridge Receivables	30%	17%
Purchase a Franchise	0	3
Machinery, Equipment, Vehicles, Computers	34	41
Market a New Product	2	1
Back Taxes	1	2
Inventory	24	25
Supplies & Materials	18	7
Purchase Real Estate	4	10
Build a New Building	5	5
Expand Existing Location	4	3
Move or Open New Location	0	4
Leasehold Improvements or Build-out	11	12
Research	1	1
Establish Line of Credit	10	10
Start a New Business	-	16
Buy Out Another Business	4	9
Buy Out a Partner	0	1
Facilitate a Buy/Sell	7	7
Restructure Debt	13	11
Hire Employees	19	6

Source: Hamlin, Roger E. 1998. *The Capital Access Program: An Evaluation of Economic Benefit.* Lansing, MI: The Michigan Jobs Commission.

Market Area. Business owners in the Michigan study were asked to describe the market area for their product or service. Responses were categorized as (1) international, (2) national, (3) Michigan, and (4) local. Responses differed dramatically by size of business. Nearly 60 percent of the larger businesses indicated their market was national or international, while about 73 percent of the smaller businesses indicated a state or local market. In this categorization, businesses that sold nearly all of their product to a local company doing business internationally would be classified as linked to an international market.

Purpose of the Loan. The Michigan interviews investigated reasons for CAP loans. Table 4.2 shows the percentage of businesses that claim each purpose or use-of-loan proceeds in the Michigan study. One loan may relate to more than one use category, so the sums of the categories are greater than 100 percent (Hamlin 1998).

Table 4.3
Loan Characteristics by Size of Business

business size	% fixed int.	% variable int.	median fixed int. rate	median var.rate (over NY prime)	% line of credit	% term loans	median maturity
Sales ≥ $1 M	47	53	9.91	1.60	43	57	40 mo.
Sales < $1 M	61	39	10.28	1.99	30	70	46 mo.

Source: Hamlin, Roger E. 1998. *The Capital Access Program: An Evaluation of Economic Benefit.* Lansing, MI: The Michigan Jobs Commission.

The meaning of some of the categories needs more explanation. "*Bridge Receivables*" refers to specific situations where (1) rapid growth, (2) unusual works in progress, or (3) an abnormally large contract created an acute and temporary need for cash to complete work. In at least two cases where a company made a rapid transition from a local operation to serving a national or international market, owners discovered that receivables were aging more than expected, causing cash-flow problems. Selection of this use of proceeds does not imply that the business needed a loan to solve general cash-flow problems.

Not all loans that were lines of credit would be included in the category *Establish a Line of Credit.* This statistic includes only those cases where a business took out the loan specifically to establish a line of credit so as to have it available when needed. In some cases, despite paying the CAP fees to establish the line, the account was never fully drawn down. In one case it was never used.

Facilitate a Buy/Sell Agreement refers to buying or selling a business. One example is where the seller is paying off a "floor plan" inventory loan to facilitate the clean purchase of the business. This kind of loan is typically not allowed under other government incentive loan programs.

Interest and Term. In general, term loans were reported to have fixed interest rates, and lines of credit had variable rates. As can be seen from Table 4.3, median interest rates vary by size of firm. A primary difference between the two Michigan samples was that the larger businesses tended to receive lines-of-credit loans with variable rates under CAP, and the smaller businesses were more likely to have term loans with fixed interest rates.

Table 4.4
Percentage of CAP Loans Requiring Various Forms of Collateral and Personal Guarantees in Michigan

item	business size category- -->	Larger (sales ≥ $1 M)	Smaller (sales < $1 M)
		%	%
direct collateral		**31**	**37**
additional assets	% yes --->	**74**	**60**
What-> 1st security lien on general business assets		43	34
receivables		29	17
inventory		15	15
business equipment		19	12
business real estate		9	6
personal guarantee	% yes --->	**92**	**79**
What-> general personal guarantee		84	71
2nd mortgage on home		30	23
assignment of life insurance		11	5
other real estate owned personally		5	3

Source: Hamlin, Roger E. 1998. *The Capital Access Program: An Evaluation of Economic Benefit.* Lansing, MI: The Michigan Jobs Commission.

Collateral and Security. Direct collateral is the collateralizing of the items purchased with the proceeds of the loan such as real estate or long-life equipment. Examples of indirect or additional collateral are when the business gives the bank a first lien on inventory, receivables, additional equipment, additional real estate, or general business assets.

For the larger-business sample in the Michigan study, the use of direct collateral was not large (31 percent). A high percentage of loans were lines of credit. Use of additional collateral was common (74 percent) and depended on the nature of the business. A retailer of consumer durable goods would be asked for a lien on inventory, a manufacturer would be required to offer a lien on machinery, and a professional firm would pledge all receivables. Many businesses did not seem to be clear about what they had pledged as collateral and could not find documentation. They often said they left such matters up to their accountant. Table 4.4 shows the percentage of loans that required various forms of direct and indirect collateral (Hamlin 1998).

Bankers who were interviewed about *Personal Guarantees* indicated that nearly all CAP borrower-participants would have to pledge personal assets. The question was raised, "If a borrower were in such a good collateral position so as not to need to pledge a personal guarantee, why would he/she need to participate in the Capital Access Program?" Ninety-one percent of the larger firm sample in Michigan and 79 percent of the smaller companies indicated they had to make personal guarantees (Hamlin 1998). The table shows the use of personal assets as guarantees of the loan (Avery, Bostic, and Samolyk 1998). The larger firms showed higher use of personal assets in every case. While this may seem illogical, one reason is that the type of loan taken out by the larger firms, unsecured lines-of-credit, required more back-up collateral.

Bankers differed on their use of *home second mortgages as business collateral.* One banker said, "nearly 25 percent of CAP loans utilize second mortgages." Another banker indicated that nearly all term loans of more than $300,000 would require a home second mortgage. A third employee at a participating bank divulged they would "take a second mortgage on a home as business collateral when it is available, but, with equity access loans, seldom is enough equity left to make it worthwhile." The interview of businesses in Michigan indicated that about 30 percent of the larger firms and about 23 percent of the smaller businesses had to pledge the equity in their home as collateral for their CAP loans (Hamlin 1998).

Attitudes about having the death benefits of a *life insurance* policy assigned to the bank differed greatly between banks. One lender said that nearly 40 percent of all their CAP loans utilize this form of protection. Another bank indicated, "waiting for someone to die doesn't make for a good way to recover loan losses." About 11 percent of the larger companies and about 5 percent of the smaller businesses had to transfer the death benefits of their life insurance as a part of their loan acquisition (Hamlin 1998).

Other Fees, Terms, and Conditions of CAP Loans. In all but a few cases, interviewed businesses indicated that they could not remember and/or had no record of significant additional bank fees or points being charged on the amount of the loan that participated in the Capital Access Program. Bankers generally said they did not charge additional fees on the CAP amount, but one lender said they almost always add another one-half percent to CAP loans.

Other than standard financial reports and inventory requirements, few businesses reported other terms and conditions of their loan. Some that were listed by interviewees included: (1) tying interest rates and/or line-of-credit limits to inventory or receivable measures; (2) pledging certifi-cates of deposit as collateral; (3) requiring cosigners; (4) demanding that all of the borrower's banking business be moved to the lending bank; (5) freez-ing savings accounts and/or requiring additional deposits to savings accounts; (6) releasing home second mortgages if the loan is paid regularly down to a designated balance; (7) rewriting the borrower's will (Hamlin 1998).

Larger Loan Packages. Was the CAP portion of a loan a key compo-nent in leveraging a larger financial package? The Michigan study asked each business whether other components of a financial package were exe-cuted at the same time as the CAP loan. Forty-seven percent of the larger businesses and 37 percent of the smaller businesses indicated the CAP loan was instrumental in leveraging significant additional financial capital. The ability of CAP loans to attract other capital is an impor-tant objective that allows the program to produce greater rates of growth and employment. Among those loans with larger financial packages, the actual financing was seven times the CAP share. Average loans of $114,000 to the larger businesses were producing average pack-ages of $710,000. For smaller businesses, average loans of approximately $47,000 leveraged packages of $255,000. Overall, $18,000,000 in loans among interviewed businesses produced $36,000,000 in total financing. Extrapolating the interview results to the entire population of loans, this means the CAP program was instrumental in providing well over one-half billion dollars in total small business finance from a variety of sources from 1988 through 1996 in Michigan. Several common finan-cial packages emerged from the interviews. Some are described below (Hamlin 1998).

The simplest of these is when only part of a single loan participated in the Capital Access Program. For example, assume a $400,000 line of credit may be offered to a business if it is willing to put $100,000 of it in the Capital Access Program. This might mean that the business would pay CAP fees of 3 percent on only the $100,000 portion of the loan for a total of $3,000 in fees. The remainder of the loan might be subjected to regular bank fees but would not be backed by the loan loss reserve fund.

Sixteen percent of the larger businesses interviewed said that their CAP loans were split such that only part was included in the program. Eight percent of the smaller businesses reported the same. Based on interviews with banks, one would expect that these percentages would be higher. One banker indicated that, for loans over $50,000, nearly half were split in this way. Another lender said that the maximum amount that they allow to be "put in the program per banking relationship" is $200,000. This means that all CAP loans with that bank over $200,000 must be only partially included. A third bank indicated that a high percentage of CAP loans have split participation.

One reason for this split, according to the lenders, is that a business might be eligible for a conventional loan in every other respect but some aspect of the loan creates a special risk or a hole in collateral coverage. An example would be a loan for the purchase of computers that is amortized over five years. Since the computers drop in value faster than the loan is paid off, a gap in collateral coverage emerges in the out years. Therefore, an amount would be put in the Capital Access Program equal to the gap. The alternative in this case would be to finance the purchase conventionally with only a one- or two-year term. This latter arrangement might endanger the company's cash flow and restrict growth, however.

Often the CAP loan will leverage a larger bank loan offered at the same time. A combination of a term loan for new machinery and a line of credit for daily operations is common where one of the two loans participates in CAP. About 42 percent of larger businesses had packages involving both a CAP loan and another bank loan, and 17 percent of the smaller businesses had such a package.

In four percent of all interview cases, the execution of a buy/sell agreement to purchase a business involved a land contract between the buyer and the seller. A bank in these cases offered a Capital Access Program-backed loan to provide financing for the down payment and/or working capital to operate the business. In these cases the businesses expressed that the CAP loan was critical to swing the deal, even though it was only a small part of the total financial package. The reason for using CAP was that the land contract holder held a primary lien on most business assets leaving a poor loan-to-value ratio for the bank loan.

About eight percent of the loans studied in the Michigan larger-firm sample and three percent of the smaller-firm sample combined the CAP loan with some *other incentive program*. Typically this was an SBA 7(a) loan. In at least one case, the CAP loan provided working capital for a business that was constructing a new building using SBA 504 financing. Incentives also listed were local tax abatements and the Federal Trade Readjustment Act.

Refinancing. About a quarter of all CAP loans are refinanced according to the Michigan interviews. Of the loans that are refinanced, about 67 percent of the businesses indicated that they paid more CAP fees. Many could not remember and/or find records indicating whether additional CAP fund deposits were required. Only two of the businesses interviewed understood that they might be eligible to borrow again, up to the same amount at the same bank, without paying additional fees. Few indicated that new conditions were placed on refinanced or recast CAP loans. Interviewed bankers said that this would be uncommon unless situations changed dramatically.

Evaluation of CAP

Community Perspective

Capital Access Programs have five notable properties as public policy, according to the U.S. Treasury. First, CAP loans generally are not intended to "crowd out" loans that the private sector would otherwise make. Since borrowers are always able to shop around to see whether another bank would lend without requiring the CAP premium, borrowers, in choosing a CAP loan, signal that they are unable to find comparable funding elsewhere. It is hoped that in this way CAPs do not supplant unsubsidized loans made by the private sector but rather leverage traditional lenders to make capital available to otherwise sidelined entrepreneurs (U.S. Treasury1998).

Second, Capital Access Program loan decisions are made by those with the best information available—the private lenders and borrowers (U.S. Treasury1998).

Third, CAPs attempt to balance the incentives of the borrower, the bank, and the state. Private incentives encourage CAP loans up to the loss level provided by the reserve fund. Banks would be disinclined to set the CAP premium too high and miss the opportunity to approve a greater number of profitable loans. Yet, the bank is induced to underwrite loans rigorously. Banks must absorb any losses that exceed the CAP reserve account protection (U.S. Treasury1998).

Fourth, public fund leverage of private capital is potentially large, and the state's risk is fixed. If the state matches a borrower and bank contribution of 5 percent of the loan amount, its contribution is backing the bank to make a loan that is 20 times larger than the state investment. Moreover, the government does not carry any contingent liability for potential future losses, as it would for a 7(a) guaranteed loan (U.S. Treasury 2001).

Fifth, the program is easy for the public agency to administer. Daily administration involves sending the matching premiums to banks' reserve funds as new loans are enrolled, marketing the program to banks, and keeping minimal records. Some states report that less than one FTE is needed to administer their program (U.S. Treasury1998). The average staff required appears to be about 1.5 full-time equivalent employees (U.S. Treasury 2001). In contrast, government loan guarantee programs often require staffing of loan review officers, record keepers, workout officers, legal professionals, and supervisors (U.S. Treasury1998).

CAP Performance Related to Policy Objectives

Loan Growth. Growth in lending nationwide would imply that the program is at least mechanically successful. CAP lending grew rapidly in the three years ending in 1998. The loan rate flattened somewhat in 1999 and then showed signs of renewed growth in 2000. CAP growth rates are consistent across the country. Of the twenty states surveyed with CAPs, only three state programs grew less than 10 percent during 1999, while the growth rates in five states were in excess of 40 percent. Pennsylvania and Colorado have been operating since 1994 and 1993 respectively and continue to achieved annual growth rates above 40 percent (U.S. Treasury 2001). The only years that the aggregate national program's growth slowed were in 1991 and 1999. Each of these years represented the early stages of a national economic downturn (Hamlin 1998).

Data show no evidence that CAP demand is saturated. First, the expansion of existing programs is generating more volume increases than the creation of new programs. Although two states started programs in 1997, 96 percent of 1997 new loan volume came from existing programs. Second, although the largest programs are most likely to tap-out demand, they continued through 2000 to extend the largest volume of new loans (U.S. Treasury 2001). However, the Michigan legislature has preliminarily decided to phase its program out, which could have a major effect on future growth nationwide.

Appropriateness of Loans. Is the Capital Access Program serving "almost bankable" situations? This question is basic to the theory of governmental involvement in loan insurance. Are CAP businesses really too risky for conventional financing? Or, conversely, are banks using the program to generate higher fees and greater protection without serving a broader market? Critics claim the latter, even though proponents lay out the theoretical logic behind the concept.

Only one study has ever addressed this question. Through a complex methodology, the aforementioned Michigan CAP study assessed this issue loan by loan. Several factors taken together contribute to an assessment of this question for each loan. They included (1) an assessment of the loan's terms and conditions, (2) the clarity of communication between the bank and the borrower about risk, and (3) the criticality of the loan to business success (Hamlin 1998).

One question asked of the Michigan interviewees was, "Have you been turned down for conventional financing?" About 72 percent of the Michigan respondents answered affirmatively, although no rule requires a turndown. A second issue was whether special risk factors were clear to the borrower and the lender. About one-fourth of the businesses said that the bank gave no explanation as to why CAP participation was important. Yet, in all but eight percent of the cases, the businesses understood the risk factors, and/or they were obvious from analysis of financials.

In several cases the business itself was financially sound and could have been eligible for a conventional loan for some purposes, but the situation of the studied loan justified CAP participation. In these cases, the issue was not the soundness of the business balance sheet, but the nature of the loan that involved additional risk. An example is where a special opportunity arises. One business was offered an unusually larger contract. The business had sound financials and banking history, but responding to the new opportunity stretched the business' cash and collateral beyond the normal bankable range. Yet, the special opportunity offered by the large contract was what the business needed to rise to a new level of operation. Financing such an opportunity seems an appropriate use of the program, and, in fact, represents a situation that generates the greatest economic gain for a state.

According to the results of the study, in the vast majority of cases, (approximately 88 percent according to the sample results) the loans that participated in the program were appropriate. This was based on borrower interviews, lender interviews, and separate analysis of the loan. This means they would not have been or should not be made conventionally. CAP was causing banks to stretch their lending to middle-risk situations. Banks were not using the program to reduce the risk of conventional financing. Each loan had at least one special risk factor that put it into the "almost bankable" category rather than "bankable" category. About 22 percent of all interviewed businesses indicated that they could not have obtained financing without CAP and would have gone out of business without the loan (Hamlin 1998). This number was based solely on their perception.

Whether the loans were appropriate in the sense of being appropriate to the developmental stage of the business and the entrepreneur is a more difficult question.

Job Creation and Retention. Often the most important issue for public policy makers when they fund economic development programs is jobs. Twelve states provided data on the number of jobs created or retained through CAP lending. Calculating the amount of CAP loan dollars per job in these twelve states shows a significant variation, from $30,000 per job in one state to $3,600 per job in another (Treasury 2001). Such job retention and creation numbers are self-reported by the borrower and by the state, and, except for the Michigan study, these figures were not independently reviewed. Applying the average employment effect for the five reporting states across the 20 states with operating CAPs suggests that as many as 90,000 jobs may have been created or retained as a result of Capital Access Programs. Assuming that banks make CAP loans twenty times the size of the state contribution and that, on average, $10,000 in CAP lending creates or retains one job (the average of the five reporting states), then one job is created or retained for each $550 state contribution to CAP reserves. This is far better than most other government-involved lending programs (U.S. Treasury1998), such as those discussed in other sections of this chapter.

The Michigan study scrutinized job creation carefully through site visits, in-depth interviews and analysis of financials. It also concluded that the existence of the program has generated jobs and economic growth that would not have occurred without the program (Hamlin and Duma 1999).

On the surface a program creates jobs in two ways. One is when new businesses are successfully created, and the second is when existing firms are induced to grow. For the population of all loans in Michigan from 1988 to 1996, more than 3,000 jobs were generated in the state by the Capital Access Program through the creation of new businesses. The total number of new employment positions was 14,000 jobs created by growth attributed to the Capital Access Program

Would firms go out of business or decline without loans? About 23 percent of the Michigan businesses indicated they would have closed operation without the CAP loan. Another 18 percent said they would have experienced severe decline. One could argue that if a business would have failed or declined without the Capital Access Program loan, then CAP helped to retain jobs. These jobs are as important as newly created jobs. Extrapolating interview figures to the total loan population, over 16,000 jobs were retained in Michigan by CAP from 1988 to 1996. Combining the three items mentioned above, 33,000 jobs were created or retained in Michigan because of the help given to small businesses by the Capital Access Program between 1988 and 1996. This estimate resulted in a ratio of $10,299 of lending per job or $390 of state contributions to loan loss reserve pools per job, even better than the national estimates (Hamlin 1998).

The measurement of job creation and retention is complicated and controversial. In a weak economy with high unemployment, nearly any new job may be seen as important. Most government incentive programs were implemented in the period from 1972 to 1992 when the economy suffered periodic high unemployment due to recessions, oil shocks, and restructuring. During periods of low unemployment when labor shortages plague many industries, the benefits of job creation can be more selective. In the mid-1990's most businesses reported difficulties in finding "good quality" employees. If a business fails in that economy, other companies might hire its employees.

Oversupply of firms in one industry may also complicate the analysis. If a pizza delivery business were to fail and lay off its employees, the jobs lost to that business would not be lost to society. In a full-employment economy, other pizza delivery businesses would fill the void, and replace the lost jobs. A true calculation of job creation and job retention to society may, therefore, be business cycle and industry dependent.

While the discussion in the previous paragraphs suggests that true job creation might be lower than the raw numbers or the simple analyses indicate, other approaches suggest that one job created may be worth more than one. Various forms of economic base analyses suggest that a multiplier magnifies the creation of some kinds of jobs. Economic base theory divides businesses into two categories, basic and non-basic. Basic businesses are those that export goods and services to places outside of the reference community and therefore bring wealth into the community. This wealth is then recycled within the community as the employees of basic businesses spend their paychecks on local services. This system has some leaks as local service businesses and local consumers buy some of their goods from the outside world.

The multiplier concept says that the income brought into a state by such "export" businesses must be multiplied by some coefficient to determine its true impact on the state's employment. The multiplier coefficient will depend on the amount of leakage in the system and will vary over time. The multiplier is very difficult to measure given current data sources.

Assuming the multiplier for Michigan has a conservatively estimated value of three, then for every person employed making products for markets beyond the state's borders, two additional local service jobs would also be created. From this perspective, subsidizing the creation of local service businesses has little worth for economic development and long-term employment since, by definition, local service businesses bring no wealth into the state. Furthermore, the theory implies that local service businesses will happen whether they are assisted or not.

On the other hand, industrial jobs and employment in multistate service organizations cause a market for local service businesses. Any activity is considered export or basic if it brings wealth into the state, even if the good or service is purchased in the state. Tourism and interstate banking are examples of export industries. Likewise, an exclusive local supplier of a basic industry might also be considered an indirect exporter, such as an automobile-parts supplier.

Are the jobs created and retained by CAP loans basic or non-basic, and what effect does the Capital Access Program have on state job creation from this perspective? Data for this kind of analysis are not available for most economic development program studies, but the CAP research might shed some light. To estimate employment effects of the Capital Access Program under the economic base philosophy, the study asked interviewed businesses to identify the market area for their product or service. The researchers eliminated from the calculation all firms with only in-state markets. For those companies serving out-of-state markets, they took the same job creation and retention figures calculated previously, using the same rules for such estimates, and then multiplied them by the multiplier 3. Using this method, 76,000 jobs resulted from the Capital Access program from 1988 through 1996. This is one job for every $3,800 of loans or one job for every $129 of state contribution to loan loss reserve pools (Hamlin and Duma 1999).

Are the numbers of jobs created enough to justify state involvement? Table 4.5 shows the amount of loans per job created or retained and the state contribution to loan loss reserve pools per job created or retained, using each of the previously discussed measures of job creation. As can be seen, any way it is measured, the Capital Access Program achieves a high leverage of benefits per dollar of commitment in comparison to other economic development programs.

Economic and Job Diversity. While each is valuable in its own way, all of the approaches to job-growth estimation oversimplify a complex world. One danger, for example, of diminishing the importance of local service businesses (as called for in the economic base approach) is that some such businesses may invent new methods and become so successful that they expand into an interstate market, thus moving from a designation of non-basic to basic. A CAP loan may be critical in facilitating that growth. This

94 FINANCING SMALL BUSINESS IN AMERICA

Table 4.5
Loan Amount and Contribution Needed to Create One Job in Michigan

business size category- -->	Larger (sales ≥ $1 M)	Smaller (sales < $1 M)
item		
est. net average job change per business	8.87	2.45
est. avg. jobs attributed to CAP - simple analysis	20.88	3.18
est. avg. jobs attributed to CAP - economic base analysis	49.06	3.45
CAP loan amt. per est. attributed job - simple	5,462.00	12,299.00
CAP loan amt. per est. attributed job - economic base	2,206.00	5,206.00
CAP avg. reserve contrib. per est. attrib job- simple	178.00	418.00
CAP avg. reserve contrib. per est. attrib job - economic base	74.00	180.00

Source: Hamlin, Roger E. 1998. *The Capital Access Program: An Evaluation of Economic Benefit.* Lansing, MI: The Michigan Jobs Commission.

was exactly the scenario for several of the businesses interviewed in the Michigan study (Hamlin 1998).

Rather than calculating job creation and retention, state policy might better ensure that an opportunity for growth and expansion exists across industries and across the spectrum of risk. Thus, a diverse set of entrepreneurs with varied skills and products can be available to respond to changing economic conditions and fluctuating markets. In this way, the marketplace will determine who thrives and grows.

From this point of view, the CAP has been highly successful. The flexibility of the program has promoted business growth in a wide variety of industries, sizes, and ages and serves a broad segment of the risk/reward spectrum. Without the Capital Access Program or something like it serving "almost bankable" situations, many businesses would be shut out of the opportunity to compete.

Promotion of economic diversity is a particular strength of the Capital Access Program. Businesses assisted by the program come from nearly every industry and size category. They also ranged from new start-ups to mature companies. The mélange of uses of loan proceeds and the divergent ways that the loans have contributed to business success reflect this diversity. This variety is also a consequence of and proof of CAP's flexible, unbureaucratic structure and the intended reliance on market forces to determine outcomes. Banks of varying sizes and approaches use the Capital Access Program in different ways depending on the needs of their local market.

Tax Revenue Generation. The revenues that state and local governments received because of this economic growth far out-stripped any state cost of the program, regardless of the estimating method used.

Overall, combining conservative estimates of the impact on state income tax, state sales tax, the Michigan Single Business Tax, and the local property and income tax, CAP can be credited with producing approximately $150,000,000 of tax revenues annually. This compares with an average annual contribution to the loan loss reserve pools of less than $1,500,000 or one percent of the benefits (Hamlin 1998).

Performance in Lending to Specific Groups. Of the state and local programs surveyed by the U.S. Treasury, nine augmented their CAP contributions for targeted groups or areas. Ten did not (U.S. Treasury 1998). Four states targeted Enterprise or Empowerment Zones and four targeted on the basis of other geographical areas in need. Four states augmented their contributions for minority-owned businesses and two for female-owned businesses. One state targeted disabled-owned businesses (U.S. Treasury 2001). All but two of these states targeted by increasing their matching contribution to a bank's reserve fund, usually by 1.5 or 2 times their ordinary match. Connecticut targets by providing a 20 percent supplemental loan guarantee for certain urban areas, and Colorado augmented its contributions by setting a minimum percentage reserve fund contribution for its targeted groups.

No objective study has investigated whether targeting works, and/or whether targeting damages the overall effectiveness of the program. Although national data are very limited, some states reported data showing that—whether the state targets specific groups or not—significant percentages of CAP loans are reaching low- and moderate-income areas as well as minority and female borrowers (U.S. Treasury 1998). Michigan's program has not targeted, and analysis does not support the national conclusion (Hamlin 1998).

According to its own definitions of "distressed areas," Oregon data showed that 30.4 percent of their CAP loans have been made in low- and moderate-income areas. Wells Fargo Bank, which had originated 72 percent of all CAP loan volume in California, made 28.1 percent of its loans to census tracts with low to moderate incomes (U.S. Treasury 2001). For these two states, average loan size in the low-to-moderate income areas is roughly equivalent to the average for all borrowers. In Oregon, the average loan size for low- and moderate-income areas is 7 percent smaller than the state average, while Wells Fargo loans to these census tracts are actually 7 percent larger on average (U.S. Treasury 1998).

Based on self-reported data, in Illinois 24.8 percent and in Wisconsin 28.9 percent of all loans went to minority entrepreneurs in 1997. Comparing these figures with the percentage of businesses that are minority owned in these states showed that CAP lending reached a higher proportion of these businesses. In Illinois 9.3 percent of businesses are minority owned compared to 2.5 percent in Wisconsin. Wisconsin's CAP does not specifically target minority-owned businesses (U.S. Treasury 1998).

Of the seven programs across the country that reported isolated lending data for female-owned businesses, the percentage of female borrowers ranges from a low of 17 percent in Vermont to a high of 34.8 percent in Wisconsin. According to the 1992 Census of Enterprises, in all five of these states, females own 33 to 35 percent of the state's firms. The average loan size for females ranges from 78 percent to 90 percent of the state average (U.S. Treasury 2001). These figures seem to indicate that female-owned businesses are underrepresented in receiving assistance from CAP.

Michigan does not collect data on the ethnic status of borrowers, so the study sample was the only source of information. Among the interviewees, 5 percent of the loans to the larger businesses went to minority-owned and -operated businesses. This figure was 10 percent for the smaller-sales business sample. The same figures for women ownership were about 6 percent for the larger businesses and 18 percent for the smaller-business sample. Michigan's CAP does not target these groups in any way. Relying on bank leadership as it does, and responding to market forces, the Michigan CAP does not assist these groups proportionally to their numbers (Hamlin 1998).

Active Marketing of the CAP. Many of the largest programs report that regular marketing is important, particularly in the initial stages of the program. Marketing to banks appears to be most important, while marketing to borrowers and others was less important in developing a high-volume CAP (U.S. Treasury 1998). The Michigan study indicated that neither borrowers nor economic-development service providers knew much about CAP unless introduced to the program by a banker (Hamlin 1998). Massachusetts, Michigan, New Hampshire, and others emphasize the importance of reaching out to banks individually, not just informing banks of the CAP's existence. States claim that CAP should be understood as a banker's tool for expanding business lending, not as a subsidy for businesses (U.S. Treasury 1998).

Lender Perspective

Different banks use CAPs to make different types of loans. For example, some banks use CAPs to target a new customer base of small businesses.

Other banks use CAPs for the unsecured portion of a financing package in which the bank will also provide some conventional secured financing. Under CAPs, banks decide how to deploy the risk-protection afforded by the loan loss reserve.

The small business community cites the financing of start-up businesses as an important need not fully satisfied by the private market. The available data appear to show that CAPs can address some of this need. Massachusetts reports that almost 18 percent of its CAP loans went to start-up businesses. In Illinois the same figure was almost 15 percent of CAP loans. This might suggest that start-ups are a market niche suitable to the CAP product (U.S. Treasury1998).

In the Michigan study, interviews with bankers revealed that their attitudes about using CAP for start-ups varied. One of the lenders at a smaller participating bank suggested that financing start-ups is an excellent use of CAP. Another community-based bank said "facilitating start-ups is our role in the community, and CAP is a perfect tool for that." A business loan vice president at one of the largest banks using the program said that his bank seldom financed start-ups in any form and indicated that they did not consider CAP an appropriate vehicle. He said the SBA 7(a) program is used more often than CAP to finance start-up businesses.

In California, a distinguishing characteristic of CAP lending is its use for working capital, another need often cited by small businesses but difficult to accommodate under other credit programs. A significant 56 percent of California's CAP lending is for working-capital revolving lines of credit, and 30 percent is for working-capital term loans. The concentration in working capital may be due to the deference CAPs give to the banks' judgment of the borrowers' creditworthiness; the preponderance of revolving facilities may be due to CAPs' straightforward loan administration.

Adequate State Appropriations for the CAP. Some state CAPs receive only limited appropriations. Of the twelve states that provided information on their funding, eight are limited either through a one-time appropriation or through an annual ceiling. Colorado and Oregon actually hit their limits in 1997, and Colorado suspended its program until new funding was obtained. Oregon kept its program operating uninterrupted by transferring funds from other budget sources. Michigan has stopped appropriations for the program (Czarnecki 2002). Even if a state is not hitting its funding limit, low funding may discourage banks from joining the program given lenders' need to make a volume of loans sufficient to build an adequate loss reserve. Some banks reported that they chose not to participate in a state's CAP because it was funded at too low a level to be able to offer the CAP product throughout their entire state branch network or to build up a sufficient reserve account. Three of the four states that reported no funding limits are also among the largest programs in the country: California, Massachusetts, and New Hampshire (U.S. Treasury1998).

Borrower Perspective

From the entrepreneur's perspective, what changes does the small business experience because of the CAP loan?

Change in Employment. The Michigan study's interviews of businesses with $1,000,000 or more in sales determined that businesses had on average about 28 employees per business just before the CAP loan. The average three months after the loan's closing was still approximately 29 per business. These are all net figures. Employment declines (including those businesses that went out of business) were subtracted from gains. Few businesses (20 percent) listed hiring new employees as a reason for taking out the loan or as a use of loan proceeds. Only six percent said that the loan contributed to business success by allowing the business to hire employees. Seldom was the loan a response to a situation that would cause immediate job creation. The larger businesses reported a net gain of approximately 9 employees per business over a three-year period following the loan. Average employment per firm increase by approximately 32 percent (Hamlin 1998).

Although the magnitudes are different, the pattern is similar for businesses with sales of less than $1,000,000. Net employment for the small business sample increased from an average of five employees to six employees three months after the loan but increased about 50 percent after three years (Hamlin 1998).

As reported in the section on community impact, overall employment gains for the state attributable to the CAP were substantial. Although businesses are not borrowing to increase their labor force, the end result of greater business success after three years is greater employment levels for the community.

Change in Sales. Net increases in sales were more dramatic than the increases in employment. For Michigan businesses with sales of $1,000,000 or more at the time of the loan, sales increased an average of $1,162,000 per business or about 44 percent in three years. For the smaller companies sales increased $304,000 or 115 percent. Like the employment data presented above, this is a net calculation, including those businesses that declined, and, at this stage of the analysis, does not imply that CAP directly caused either the gains or the losses (Hamlin 1998).

Change in Debt. Among interviewed firms in the larger-business sample, debt increased by about $328,000 per business in the 36 months after the loan. This includes all debt, not just CAP loans. This is a sizable increase that amounts to almost one-third of the sales increases. For the smaller businesses debt increased by an average of $88,000 per business or between one-third and one-fourth of the sales increases (Hamlin 1998).

Change in Property Tax. Because many of the CAP loans were used for new machinery and equipment, and some were used for buildings or expansions, property tax payments increased significantly shortly after closing the loan. Annualized, personal and real property-tax payment increases resulting from the CAP loan packages in Michigan were about $5,000 and $2,600 per business for the larger and smaller size groups respectively (Hamlin 1998).

Purpose Accomplished? Three months after the loan 99 percent of the larger Michigan businesses and 93 percent of the smaller businesses said the purpose for taking out the loan was accomplished. Three years after the loan, a lower percentage felt the purpose was accomplished (89 percent for larger, 84 percent for smaller). This reflects that problems set in over time. For example, if they took out a line-of-credit loan to solve a cash-flow problem, their cash flow may have been good after three months, but deteriorated later. Yet, the satisfaction rate among interviewed businesses was high. This calculation includes those entrepreneurs researchers interviewed whose businesses ultimately terminated operation.

Loan's Contribution to Long Term Success. Table 4.6 presents the percentage of Michigan business owners who claim each listed way in which the CAP loan contributed to their business' success. The columns do not add to 100 percent because a business could list more than one. The reasons were numerous and the spread across them was great. This table illustrates the variety of ways in which the Capital Access Program serves the small business community.

Starting or buying a business was clearly important to the smaller-business sample (29 percent). "Allowing for business growth" was most important for the bigger businesses (56 percent). The CAP loans also helped businesses raise other financial capital, reduce costs, start a new product line, and respond to special opportunities or situations. In many cases, companies were able to grow or maintain their level of business because the Capital Access Program allowed them to buy needed equipment. Expanding space through new buildings, physical additions, or new locations also helped businesses succeed (see also Table 4.2, Use of Proceeds: Percent of Michigan Interviewees by Size of Business) but to a

Table 4.6
How CAP Loans Contributed to the Success of Michigan Businesses: Percentage of Interviewees Responding to Each Category

"The loan contributed to the success of thebusiness because it allowed us to:	Larger Businesses sales ≥ $1 M	Smaller Businesses sales < $1 M
start or buy a business	8%	29%
start a new product line	6	11
increase inventory and selection	11	9
improve equipment	25	20
expand space	8	8
finance bigger customers	13	5
improve quality	8	8
hire more employees	6	3
take advantage of a special opportunity	10	16
gain other financial capital	20	29
reduce costs	16	14
get through a difficult period	21	18
restructure debt	14	11
Did not succeed.	6	8

Source: Hamlin, Roger E. 1998. *The Capital Access Program: An Evaluation of Economic Benefit.* Lansing, MI: The Michigan Jobs Commission.

lesser degree than the other reasons mentioned above. In general, CAP loans are not often used for "brick and mortar."

Significantly, "surviving difficult financial times" (19 percent) and "debt restructuring," (12 percent) were not listed as major ways in which a CAP loan contributed to success. These figures are particularly interesting because the nation's economy has had some rough spots during the history of the Capital Access Program. Interviews of commercial loan officers reinforced these business interview results. The bankers indicated that they did not like to use the Capital Access Program to resolve cash-flow problems or extend debt terms for businesses having problems. They indicated that such loans might be served best through SBA 7(a), if at all (Hamlin 1999).

What if CAP Did Not Exist? If the business had been turned down for conventional financing and if the Capital Access Program did not exist, what would the consequences have been for the business? As can be seen

Table 4.7
Consequences of No CAP Loan for Michigan Businesses

Consequence business size category- -->	Larger (sales ≥ $1 M)	Smaller (sales < $1 M)
business failure	27%	21%
slower growth	47	35
business decline	24	16
not buy/start business	5	21
more difficult financing	24	19
more family or partner funds	5	6
no consequence	1	11

Source: Hamlin, Roger E. 1998. *The Capital Access Program: An Evaluation of Economic Benefit.* Lansing, MI: The Michigan Jobs Commission.

in Table 4.7, between one-fourth and one-fifth of all business owners felt they would have failed. Another 21 percent of the owners of the smaller businesses said they would not have bought the business or started it because the financing was a critical part of the start-up. Slower growth or business decline was considered a probable outcome, with 47 percent of the heads of larger businesses indicating that their firm would have grown more slowly without the CAP loan. While some felt they could have obtained financing elsewhere, they felt it would be a more expensive or more difficult loan causing them to pay higher fees, higher interest rates, or use more business and personal collateral. In other words, the consequences would have been great (Hamlin 1998).

Bankers perceived the situation differently. They indicated that if there were no Capital Access Program most CAP customers would have been able to find partners or obtain money from family and friends (Hamlin 1998).

Summary

CAP is one of only a few economic development incentive programs that has been studied objectively. Study results indicate that mechanically, the program works very well. The program does perfect the marketplace for midrisk capital and does induce banks to channel funds to both new and existing small businesses. Banks, states, and borrowers generally like the program. However, the state of Michigan, moving its priorities away from small business development, is phasing out the nation's first program. The program does seem to meet policy objectives of promoting jobs and tax revenues with minimal governmental intervention and cost. It does this by inducing bank loan officers to stretch their loan practices to somewhat riskier loans, with insurance support.

The program's primary weakness flows from its strength. It is a program run by banks. The program does not replace the collateral-oriented lending practices of business loan officers: it enhances them. The program does not move the entrepreneurial development system toward a practice that assists entrepreneurs and businesses to become more successful. Rather, the program is used heavily by banks to plug collateral holes of almost bankable businesses.

While the program clearly serves small businesses (even when the rules do not limit business or loan size) the research is unclear whether targeted, disadvantaged groups and places are well served. This includes women- and minority-owned businesses and businesses in declining communities. While some Capital Access Programs use targeting incentives, it is not clear whether targeting works and whether targeting creates other problems.

If better integrated into a comprehensive process of enterprise development, the program can be a valuable component.

LOANS WITH KICKER FEATURES: BIDCOS

The Kicker Concept

One approach to providing debt capital to small businesses is to offer a loan with a kicker. An equity kicker is an additional clause in a loan agreement that would provide some additional financial reward to the lender if the borrowing business were to become highly successful. The financial benefit is in addition to the successful repayment of the loan with interest. The reward, as the name "equity kicker" implies, is typically tied in some way to business ownership.

As a simplistic example, a borrower might offer the lender stock in the borrower's company in partial exchange for providing a loan to the company. If the borrowing company becomes highly successful, the lender receives both interest on the loan and capital gains on the stock as a reward. If the company survives but is not highly successful, the lender might still receive loan repayment and interest on the loan, but little or no capital gains on the stock. Unlike the venture capitalist, the lender's interest in the business is purely financial with little desire to own or control the company.

This approach to debt capital provision is discussed in this book because it represents another kind of middle-risk debt financing. While the lender receives additional potential financial rewards from the equity kicker, it is expected to give something in return. Two related reciprocations are (1) the lender's willingness to make a loan that is somewhat more risky than the lender would take on without the kicker, and (2) a willingness to extend somewhat more favorable terms to the borrower. In essence, the lender is sharing some of the risk of failure with the hope of sharing some of the rewards of success. The lender might be willing to undertake such a loan if the business shows exceptional growth promise despite a less-than-bankable current financial status.

Since the lender is not very interested in ownership, and since the borrowing businesses are often small and young with illiquid common stock, the simplistic approach described in the previous paragraphs is not common. A more typical approach is for the equity kicker to take the form of stock options, or warrants. These financial instruments give their owner the option to buy stock at a set price in the future. That right is extended for a set period of time with an expiration date.

This approach offers benefits to both the borrower and the lender. From the lender's point of view, if the market value of the company does improve, an option instrument will increase in relative value much more dramatically than will the underlying stock. Assume, for example, that the market value of a share of stock doubles from $21 to $42 in three months, an increase of 100 percent. An option that gives the holder the right to buy that stock at $20 per share might increase in value from approximately $1 per option to $22 per option, an increase of 2100 percent or twenty-five fold in the same period. This is because the option allows the holder, after the stock price increases, to buy the underlying share at $20, sell it at $42, and make an instant $22 per-share profit.

The option holder does not have to execute the option to benefit. The option holder never has to own the company's underlying stock. If the increase in stock value is clearly known to potential buyers of the stock, and if the holder of the option can connect with such buyers, the option holder may sell the option to this third party rather than convert or exercise the option. For a public entity, such as a local revolving loan fund, avoiding actual ownership of the company might be politically and administratively desirable.

For the borrower, providing the lender a kicker in the form of an option instead of stock offers benefits that go beyond just better loan terms. The option strategy might avoid having the lender ever be an actual owner of the company. The option holder can just sell the option as described above. Also, since options expire, the borrower can be fairly certain that the lender will be out of the equity picture at some point in time. Furthermore, if the borrowing company has little or no near-term business success, such that its stock's market value does not go up, the option value will be zero and will not be exercised. Therefore, when a company that provided an option as an equity kicker has moderate near-term success, it will be less likely to experience stock dilution than a company that provided the underlying stock as an equity kicker.

Another kind of kicker often attached to a loan is a royalty agreement. The agreement can be written so as to give the lender either a share of the revenues of one of its products or a share of the sales revenues of the entire business. While a royalty agreement may not technically be equity, it does give the lender a share in the success of the borrower.

A royalty kicker avoids some problems associated with true equity. One problem with a true equity kicker is that the kicker holder faces some of the same concerns faced by a venture capitalist. Benefits are based on company profits and/or increases in net worth. This means that an equity holder has a stake in the details of company operation, particularly its cost structure. The equity holder has difficulty protecting its interests unless it has some control over company operations. Anti-dilution clauses are used to ensure that the borrower's net worth is not diluted through stock sale or sale of assets. Also of great concern are excessive salaries or bonuses paid to principals of the company. As a result of this concern, many venture capitalists will demand some ultimate control over day-to-day business operations, something that both lenders and borrowers would like to avoid. A royalty agreement based on product revenues rather than profits or net worth reduces the lender's concern for micromanagement of the business' cost structure.

The BIDCO Program: History and Purpose

Business and Industrial Development Corporations (BIDCOs) offer another model for government intervention to promote mezzanine and midrisk financing. BIDCO programs are usually state programs. The federal government does not have a BIDCO program.

The first BIDCO was established in California in 1977. In 1985 the state of Michigan established the Michigan Strategic Fund to increase the availability of business financing in that state. One part of that effort was the creation in 1986 of BIDCOs. The Michigan program used California's as a model. Now many more states have programs, including Louisiana, Alaska, New York, Iowa, West Virginia, Missouri, Idaho, and Tennessee.

In nearly all states the term "BIDCO" refers to a non-depository financial institution that offers a broad range of financing services to businesses considered moderate risk. While considerable variation is found across states, BIDCOs often have the authority to provide consulting as well as financial services. The financing methods include both direct-collateralized or unsecured loans. They are enabled to make loans with equity features, subordinated conventional loans, direct equity investments and SBA-guaranteed loans (if the BIDCO is approved as a Small Business Administration participating lender), or a combination of financing in the same package to the same business.

BIDCOs were established to promote economic development through lending to young growth firms with moderate risk. Occasionally they lend to start-up's. Such firms are usually unappealing investments for the conservative banking industry, and may not provide a high-enough potential return on investment for venture capitalists. The BIDCO law represents a loosening of lending regulations to provide a higher level of flexibility. BIDCOs are allowed to take more risk than banks because they are not depository institutions. On the other hand, they allow a higher return on investment, because many state lending laws restrict the interest rate banks can charge.

How the Program Works

Organization and Capitalization. The BIDCO program operates at the state level. It starts with the state authorizing and legitimizing a non-bank financial intermediary organization called a Business and Industrial Development Corporation (BIDCO).

The next step is for interested parties to set up corporations with an appropriate special-purpose charter as described by the state BIDCO act. BIDCOs are typically for-profit, stockholder organizations but can also be nonprofits in some states.

The third step is for interested owners and operators to raise private capital to finance the organization. This initially involves several million dollars. The private financing generally takes the form of equity financing or stock ownership in the BIDCO corporation. Unlike banks, BIDCOs acquire their funds to make loans from equity investors, not from depositors. Those equity investments can be leveraged with borrowed funds.

The fourth step is for the incorporated and funded entity to become licensed as a BIDCO. To be licensed as a BIDCO means that the applicant must be properly incorporated as a for-profit or nonprofit, but licensing is different from and in addition to incorporation. The corporation must also demonstrate a minimum liquid net worth that will allow it to provide financial assistance. Additionally, each officer, director, or person with controlling interest will be evaluated for good character. A variety of entities may own and operate BIDCOs. These include individuals, governmental bodies, non-profit organizations, and financial institutions. The individual in control must also demonstrate good character and sound financial standing to a commissioner or financial institution's bureau of the state before a license can be issued. This same condition also applies to an acquisition or merger of BIDCOs.

The fifth step is for government to share some of the risk by assisting in the financing of the BIDCO. The state often says that it will match all private-equity investments in the BIDCO with its own equity investment. A dollar-for-dollar match up to some limit is common. Some states require two private dollars for every public dollar of equity injection.

A similar federal program authorized under the Small Business Act of the 1950's promotes the existence of Small Business Investment Corporations (SBIC). Under that program, if an organization becomes certified as an SBIC, the federal government makes low-interest loans to the SBIC to promote its ability to invest in small businesses. The state BIDCO program generally matches private-equity capital investments with public-equity capital. Often, the BIDCO must buy back the state-equity investment after a set number of years.

Small Business Lending. When a BIDCO is authorized and fully funded, it may assist small businesses with financial capital. In some states, if the state has injected equity into the BIDCO or provided other subsidies, the BIDCO may only operate in its home state, although it usually may operate statewide. Typically BIDCOs make loans of $1,500,000 or less to established small businesses with growth potential. As a stockholder-financed rather than a depository-financed lender, BIDCOs would normally look for higher-risk situations than conventional lenders. They would also seek higher rates of return than they could earn on a conventional loan. In this way, BIDCOs can increase the capital available to medium-risk small businesses. In states with usury laws, they would be exempt from usury interest limits.

BIDCOs may also make conventional loans, and may make SBA 7(a)-guaranteed loans if they are a licensed SBA lender. Some BIDCOs engage in SBA-guaranteed lending, partly to diversify their loan portfolio and partly to be able to offer a larger variety of products to their clients. Yet, most of the situations they would pursue would be too risky to gain SBA approval.

BIDCOs are allowed to engage in some practices not allowed to banks. Principal among those, for the sake of this discussion, is the ability to demand a kicker as a part of their loan agreement. Typically they require a royalty agreement, thus increasing their return on a successful investment.

BIDCOs look for a return on investment of 20 to 40 percent. According to Steven Sandstedt, CEO of Capital BIDCO, they typically structure the deal to provide a 25 percent-total return on investment, when the future success of the business is conservatively estimated. This level and method seems to be what businesses will accept. Thus, if they were able to charge a 15 percent interest rate on the loan, they would look for royalty revenues equivalent to an additional 10 percent return on the loan amount. If the loan interest were 10 percent, the BIDCO would extract a royalty that would offer an additional 15 percent return, based on a conservative estimate of future business revenues (Sandstedt 2002).

The royalty is best written against total company revenues. If the royalty is against the revenues from a particular product or part of the business' operations, then greater scrutiny of the company's books is necessary. This is to ensure that bookkeeping vagaries have not minimized the revenue postings for the product in question (Sandstedt 2002).

BIDCOs can also offer leasing services. Specifically, many are enabled "to purchase, receive, hold, lease, or otherwise acquire, or to sell, convey, mortgage, lease, pledge, or otherwise dispose of, real and personal property. Leasing plant and equipment to businesses can be seen as a kind of loan. It offers needed physical capital now in exchange for periodic payments. The ability to lease creates a unique opportunity to allow expansion of moderate-risk business clients. At the same time it offers BIDCO investors the tax benefits resulting from the depreciation of leased items" (Act 89, section 503.2.d of Michigan Public Acts of 1985).

BIDCOs are often thought of as quasi-venture capital companies. The businesses they lend to are generally fast-growth companies with some technology orientation, and BIDCO loans are often labeled growth loans. But the BIDCO is more accurately described as between a conventional lender and a venture capitalist, and the rules and goals of a BIDCO are quite different from those of either of the others.

First of all, neither the growth potential nor the uniqueness of the technology of a BIDCO client need be as great as that of a venture-capital client. Second, the amount of the investment is typically much less. BIDCOs make mezzanine loans in the range of $100,000 to $1,000,000 as opposed to the venture-capital investment of $1,000,000 to $20,000,000.

Third, venture capitalists usually take substantial equity positions in companies. Their goal is to take the company from its infancy to full scaled-up operation, producing and selling a unique technological product. The venture capitalist usually hopes to sell out its equity position at a substantial profit in three to five years, either to other investors or, alternatively, to take the company public. From the venture-capitalist point of view this process often requires that they have firm control of the reins of the company.

While a BIDCO is allowed to have an equity position in a company, the goal should not be company control. Some states in fact outlaw long-term control of a client company and require that any short-term takeover of a company be preceded by a request for permission to the state, with an explanation as to why a short-term takeover is necessary.

Asset/Receivable Financing. Recently some states have allowed BIDCOs to expand into receivable or asset-based financing. Star BIDCO of Delaware is an example. Many small businesses suffer a large lag time from the time they produce work to the time they are paid by the buyer. This problem might be particularly difficult for some service companies. For example, assume a small business concern named SBC Inc. produces a product or service and sells it to company XYZ. Also, assume company XYZ does not pay for the purchase until 90 days after delivery. The small growth business (SBC Inc.) might have to pay for employee salaries, materials and supplies, and overhead for nearly six months from the time it begins production until the time it received related revenues. This situation creates an enormous cash-flow problem.

One solution to this problem is for company SBC to sell its receivable invoices to a third party (we will call it AR Bidco), typically at a substantial discount. Company SBC then receives some revenues faster, and the third party, AR Bidco, can make a profit collecting revenues from the buyer XYZ. An option to this scenario, called asset/receivable lending, calls for the third-party lender to make a loan to Company SBC using sales invoices as collateral. AR Bidco collects a fee for the service in addition to earning interest on the loan. The loan is typically factored, meaning that the loan is only a percentage of the full value of the collateralized receivable. In these cases, a BIDCO might be the third-party lender.

To engage in receivables-based lending, the BIDCO will have to work with SBC's regular bank to get a release on the chosen receivables. This is because the bank will likely have requested a generalized commitment of company assets as a part of the indirect collateral on a previous loan. Banks sometimes don't like when receivables-based lenders "cherry pick" the most promising receivables on which to receive collateral releases. However, if the BIDCO loan is subordinated to all bank loans, the bank might appreciate the financial support its customer is receiving from the BIDCO.

Sometimes these asset-based loans are made using a standard boiler plate or loan-agreement form. Then a secondary market for the loans can be created. This operates much like the secondary market for mortgages created by a corporation like Fannie Mae. A secondary market maker (we will call it SMM Inc.) will buy and bundle asset-based loans, from the A/R lender and then sell a bond issue backed by the bundle of asset-backed loans. (All of the loans must have been made using a compatible boiler plate to avoid legal complexities.) Bundling spreads the risk associated with the bonds over many A/R loans such that the failure of one small business borrower will not destroy the value of the bond. The bonds are high-yield securities sold to the general public.

Asset-based lending can theoretically use almost any of the assets on a small business' balance sheet. Mortgage-backed securities technically represent a kind of asset-based lending since mortgage loans are assets to the lender. Other assets that can be sold or used as collateral in asset-based lending include leases, inventory, contracts, work-in-progress, or nearly any contractual guarantee that produces a future income stream that can be capitalized.

Fast-growing companies suffer growth-related cash-flow problems more than slow-growth companies. This is true, first of all, because fast-growth companies are expanding their sales and therefore increasing their receivables on sales. Second, fast-growth companies are beginning to deal with new customers that have not established a receivables history with the company. The customer base might also be spread across a larger geographic area and a larger industry spectrum. This more-complicated customer portfolio might make receivables more expensive and time consuming to collect.

Since BIDCOs are designed to provide mezzanine, midrisk financing to fast-growth companies, it might be natural for them to engage in asset-backed lending. Some feel receivables lending fits well with royalty kickers since both are sales based. In other words, the BIDCO makes a loan to a small-growth company, uses factored assets such as receivables as collateral, and attaches a royalty kicker agreement to the loan based on future sales. This combination rewards both the borrower and the BIDCO for rapid sales growth and good collection practices while providing some risk-sharing between the parties.

Consulting Services. A behavior allowed to BIDCOs in some states that is not granted to banks is for BIDCOs to provide managerial assistance to businesses and charge a consulting fee. This is again designed to allow BIDCOs to operate in a role between that of banks, which can have no equity interest in their borrowing clients and that of venture capitalists which often have substantial control over operations.

Evaluation of BIDCOs and Kicker Financing

Community Perspective

BIDCOs have continued to exist for many years and have slowly grown in number. New states are continuing to add BIDCO programs to their portfolio of economic-development initiatives. This growth would imply that they are providing a needed service. Yet, the growth has been slow, primarily because of a difficulty in raising capital. At least one state, Michigan, has started to phase out its BIDCO program. The risk/reward balance does not seem to be right in many states to attract private investors to the program. Either state governments have not yet shared enough risk, or the business community is not yet familiar enough with royalty lending. One of the complaints of Michigan BIDCO operators has been that the state law creating the program required that all BIDCOs be C corporations and did not allow limited-liability-corporation ownership. This, they claim, made it more difficult to raise capital since private investors could not gain certain tax advantages through a C corporation (Sandstedt 2002). Some BIDCOs have relied heavily on consulting fees for revenues and the addition in some states of asset-based financing and other flexible approaches has added new dimensions.

Governmental Image. Some claim that in many states the BIDCO program could never shake the image of being a governmental program. Instead of looking at BIDCOs as private companies that have been legally empowered by state law and temporarily injected with state equity, BIDCOs are perceived as slow-moving organizations burdened with government paperwork and regulation. Given that many BIDCOs were set up by governmental entities, this perception might also be held by some owner-operators of BIDCOs, many of whom never fully utilized the flexibility BIDCOs provide (Sandstedt 2002).

Little objective research has been completed on BIDCOs. Although many of the benefits of the program that will be described below are widely claimed by stakeholders, these have not been rigorously verified.

Innovation. The most innovative feature of the BIDCO system is that it institutionalizes a process for risk-sharing through royalty agreements attached to loans. Originally, when BIDCOs were first created, they were perceived of more as a venture investor. The ability to provide technical assistance through paid consulting services was seen as a more important aspect of the program. Royalty lending was originally seen as only one of many venture tools, but in some states this has become a primary activity.

Job Creation and Retention. In much the way many small business development programs would, BIDCOs can claim to create jobs. They have assisted numerous businesses and have launched some successful firms that have experienced rapid growth. It is assumed that some of these businesses would not have succeeded if the program did not exist.

The kind of firms BIDCOs assist are not generally considered to be labor intensive or to be good employers of semi-skilled workers. So, the promise of job creation is a long-term prospect resulting from the success of new and high-growth businesses rather than a direct, short-term effect of one BIDCO loan. Job retention is probably not a strong suit for the BIDCO program. It is a program designed for relatively new companies with relatively rapid growth trajectories. It is not designed for the preservation of jobs offered by slower-growth industrial firms, and it is not a program to save ailing businesses.

Economic Diversification. Because BIDCO focuses on newer growth companies and newer technologies, it should be a program that can be used to diversify a community's or state's economic base. Some states such as California have targeted their BIDCOs to certain industries so as to promote economic diversity.

Performance in Lending to Specific Groups. No evidence suggests that any state has successfully targeted their BIDCO program to promote entrepreneurial development or job creation for women or minorities. Nor have BIDCOs been used extensively to develop lagging communities. The government-incentive mechanism involved in BIDCOs does not lend itself easily to such targeting without the creation of special BIDCOs designed for that purpose.

Tax Revenue Generation. Successful businesses will create tax revenues. The kinds of development created by BIDCO financed businesses would be most beneficial to states with personal and corporate income taxes.

Cost of the Program to Government. Theoretically, if the state-equity investment in the BIDCO is bought back by the BIDCO after the prescribed number of years, the cost to the state would be very little. In addition to some state administrative expenses, costs would only be incurred when a BIDCO failed during the start-up period. No data are available on how many BIDCOs have failed across the United States.

Success at Leveraging Private Capital. Clearly a BIDCO must leverage private funding to capitalize itself. BIDCOs typically only receive an initial one-to-one equity match from government, that must be bought back. The governmental investment is therefore leveraging some private capital in the equity injection process. If BIDCOs are created by states and are successfully recycling their loan funds to generate new investments for years, then one can say that the initial state injection has been highly successful at leveraging private investment into midrisk small business lending.

Are BIDCOs leveraging private capital in the lending process? Are BIDCO loans helping to generate larger funding packages? In some states BIDCOs tend to subordinate their royalty-kicker loans to conventional bank loans or a 7(a) loan. When this happens, we know that additional private investment is being attracted to the business. However, no information indicates the extent to which BIDCOs are leveraging other capital on the loans they make.

Crowding Private Investments. On the opposite side of the discussion of the leveraging power on any governmental incentive program is whether the governmental program is crowding out, discouraging, or supplanting private investment in areas where the private sector would otherwise function on its own. Although the objective research is lacking, it appears that BIDCOs are addressing a part of the debt-capital markets that is not well served in their absence. Some of the other areas BIDCOs are getting into, such as ABS and equipment leasing, might be competing with unsubsidized private A/R businesses.

Borrower Perspective

Since BIDCOs are private non-bank lending corporations, they do not have to reveal the status of loans the way banks do. States do not have good information on BIDCO loan-failure rates.

Relationship of Lending and Providing Advice? An interesting aspect of BIDCOs is the ability of the lender to provide consulting services. This has potentially good and bad aspects with respect to enterprise development. The combination of an equity or royalty stake in the borrower, in addition to the right to provide management consulting, should foster a relationship that is different from the collateral lending focus of banks. The lender has a greater stake in the success of the borrower and a greater ability to effectuate that success. BIDCOs have tended to focus on a smaller number of businesses and have worked more closely with them than other kinds of lenders.

Research clearly shows that small businesses need greater knowledge and assistance to go along with financing, but no interviews have been conducted to determine to what degree BIDCO clients value the technical assistance they receive from BIDCOs. One reason why banks have not been given the right to provide fee-based consulting services to loan clients is to avoid conflicts of interest. Is there a chance, for example, that the management consultant might induce the business to take on more debt than it should with the BIDCO being the only possible lender?

On the other hand, the BIDCO as lender might pressure the business to take on expensive consulting services that are not that helpful. One can imagine for example, a situation in which the business becomes indebted to a BIDCO, is unable to raise private capital from other sources, and is therefore solely dependent for survival on its relationship with the BIDCO. It would therefore be susceptible to various pressures from the BIDCO staff.

Summary

Business and Industrial Development Corporations represent one more weapon in the arsenal of economic-development professionals to perfect money markets to ensure that adequate midrisk debt capital is available to small businesses. A BIDCO is a privately owned non-bank, non-depository lender that responds to market forces when making loans with little governmental oversight. Government's contribution to the process is primarily to use its powers to define and legally sanction such an organization much the way government does with banks. To diversify debt-capital markets, government provides BIDCOs with more flexible rules than are used by conventional banks. The flexibility allows BIDCOs to lend to midrisk clients. It can do this because depositor funds are not at risk. Government also shares some of the risk of starting up a BIDCO by temporarily injecting equity capital into a young BIDCO. This stock purchase must typically be bought back.

BIDCOs tend to focus on fast-growth companies and have found loans with kicker arrangements to be their niche to support those businesses. Theoretically, the potential reward from royalties allows BIDCOs to take on more risk. Some have also become involved in receivable-based lending.

Objective evaluation of BIDCOs is lacking. Anecdotally, some companies have benefited greatly from BIDCO financing and some states have successfully used BIDCOs as one small tool to help build and diversify their economic base. One the other hand, some states report slow growth in BIDCO formation, capitalization, and utilization. At least one state is phasing out its program. The reason BIDCOs have not always lived up to expectations is not clear. Perhaps government is not sharing enough risk through its initial equity injection. Perhaps not enough people have real expertise in all aspects of royalty-based lending. Perhaps businesses are not familiar enough with the concept and more marketing is needed.

Perhaps the system needs to be better tied into the conventional debt capital market system. Some BIDCOs are subsidiaries of banks. Some BIDCOs have had success subordinating their royalty financing to loans from partnering banks (see subordinated lending in the next section).

The BIDCO concept offers great potential benefit as one component of a comprehensive system of enterprise development. The concept moves away from collateral-oriented lending. It puts greater emphasis on technical assistance and closer guidance for the business. Lender success is more tied to the borrower's success. Tying BIDCOs more fully into a comprehensive enterprise-development system and enhancing the attractiveness of BIDCO investing for potential investors might help BIDCOs play a more vital role in small business success.

SUBORDINATED LENDING: CERTIFIED DEVELOPMENT CORPORATION LOANS

The Subordinated Lending Concept

A sixth way for government to induce debt capital to flow to small businesses is through subordinated lending. A loan is subordinated if another loan has a superior claim on the assets of the business. A common subordinated loan that is well known by the general public is a second mortgage on a house.

Assume that a primary lender lends 50 percent of the value of a real-estate purchase and takes a first mortgage on the property. Fifty percent of the property value is still available as collateral. Assume further that a second lender lends an amount equal to 40 percent of the property value and takes a second mortgage as collateral. The buyer must still provide 10 percent.

If, at some point in time, the borrower fails to repay the loans, the senior or superior position lender has first access to the equity in the real estate. As a part of the loan-recovery process, the lender will liquidate the property and keep enough from the sale to payoff their loan. The subordinated lender receives the amount, if any, that is left after the senior loan is fully paid.

Clearly, the subordinated lender takes a much greater risk than the primary lender. Furthermore, if the subordinated lender is willing to cover a significant portion of the value of the loan package with the subordinated loan, the subordinated loan can reduce the risk to the primary lender. In the example the second-position loan reduces the loan-to-value ratio faced by the primary lender to 50 percent, in a situation where a lender might normally be asked to lend 80 percent of the project cost.

Furthermore, if the second-position loan improves the chance of business success, as any appropriate loan should, the subordinated loan increases the chances that the primary lender will be fully repaid. And, if the addition of a subordinated loan reduces the downpayment or equity the business must contribute to the project, (say from 20 percent to 10 percent in the hypothetical example) the second-position loan will improve the business' cash flow.

Therefore, the willingness of someone to make a second-position loan could induce banks and other traditional lenders to make primary loans to middle-risk borrowers and small businesses. The entity making the second-position loan is sharing some of the risk of the business' development and, as a result, is inducing traditional debt-capital institutions to become more fully engaged in small business development without taking inappropriate risk. Some form of government or quasi-governmental organization is often the second-position lender.

The Certified Development Corporation Program: A Brief History and Purpose

A prime example of governmental involvement in second-position lending is the Certified Development Corporation (CDC) program. Authorized by Section 504 of Title V of the U.S. Small Business Act of 1958 as amended, the program allows for the creation of private corporations that may make second-position loans to small businesses for purchase of real estate or long-life equipment. The program began as Section 501. In 1983 Section 503 began, which implemented a complex subordinated debenture concept. The first organizations to jump into the program with new 503 corporations were regional-planning agencies and state economic development agencies. They generally created nonprofit corporations as subsidiaries of their territorial economic development efforts. Over the years, more for-profit corporations became involved. In 1986, Section 503 was replaced with section 504. Through the years the SBA has struggled with creating a balance between private and public goals including rigorous loan analysis versus non-bureaucratic behavior. However, the basic structure created by SBA 503 has changed little in 20 years.

The National Association of Development Companies (NADCO) indicates that from October 1986 to May 2002, 54,067 CDC loans have been approved providing $19,197,259,266 in loan proceeds (NADCO 2002). Since the 504 loan is only part of the loan package, this has amounted to $47,993,148,165 in project funding, including both the bank first mortgage and the borrower injection. SBA information indicates that, as of January 1, 2002, 1,314 loans from the 503 program were outstanding with a balance of $128,823,000. Section 504 loan data indicate that 31,136 loans with a balance of $9,468,238,000 are on the books (Hook 2002).

How the Program Works

CDC Formation and Certification. The first step is for someone to form a corporation for the purpose of engaging in 504 loan activities. The corporation may be either for-profit or nonprofit. It must have a board of directors that broadly represents the community it is to serve. It must also state its special purpose in the articles of incorporation.

The corporation must apply to the U.S. SBA for certification as a 504 lender. A specific geographic service area is specified in the application. The U.S. SBA determines that the applicant meets all of the organizational criteria and then investigates the skills, expertise, and personal character of the members of the board and officers. If approved by the SBA the corporation is certified to engage in Section 504 loan activities.

More than 280 Certified Development Companies serve communities throughout the United States (Dakota 2002). Most of the 504 corporations are nonprofit organizations. Some are set up as for-profit corporations. Many of the nonprofits are founded by and staffed by government agencies such as regional planning commissions, state departments of commerce, councils of government, or local economic-development corporations.

Examples of CDCs are the Brooklyn Certified Development Corporation, the Dakota Certified Development Corporation (Dakota CDC 2002), the Long Island Development Corporation, Enchantment Land Certified Development Corporation (Enchanted Lands CDC 2002), Pikes Peak Regional Development Corporation, and the South Bend Business Development Corporation (McKinney 2002). NADCO, the National Association of Development Companies, is a trade association of certified development corporations (NADCO 2002) and provides training, technical assistance, and other services.

The Loan Application Process. After certification, the corporation can accept loan applications from businesses in their service area. Applications are subordinated loans for real estate or long-life equipment. The applicant must be working with a bank to secure a primary loan. CDCs review the applications for eligibility, business financial condition, collateral and security, and the economic impact of the proposed project. CDCs may reject applications. If they accept an application preliminarily, and the business secures a promise of first-position bank financing in conjunction with the CDC loan, the application will be recommended to the SBA for final approval. The SBA regional or district office then reviews the applications. The decision SBA is officially making is whether to guarantee the debenture that the CDC sells to the federal government to cover the loan (see explanation below). Without the guarantee, the process cannot go forward.

Alternatively, the CDC may buy equipment or real estate and lease it to the small business. The lease behaves like a loan, and the approval process is similar to the subordinated loan. A primary difference is who may depreciate the equipment for tax purposes.

Business Eligibility. If a business can not obtain conventional financing from non-federal sources on reasonable terms, a business may qualify for 504 assistance by meeting several criteria. They are:

- The business must be a for-profit corporation, limited liability company, partnership or proprietorship, and must have a sound business purpose.
- The net worth of the business and its affiliates must not exceed $7 million. Its average net income (after taxes) must not exceed $2.5 million for the last two years (NADCO 2002).
- The project being financed must demonstrate economic impact on its community, primarily through job creating and retention (see next section).

Certain businesses are not eligible for 504 financing. These include:

- Not-for-profits (except sheltered workshops);
- Religious institutions;
- Companies whose stock in trade is money, such as stock brokerage houses, banks, and insurance companies (local for profit insurance agencies are eligible);
- Offshore facility;
- Speculative operation;
- Lobbyists; and
- Businesses with more than one-third of income derived from legal gambling.

Economic Development Requirements. SBA 504 is a community-lending program designed to improve the locality. As indicated in the previous section, the project being financed must demonstrate economic impact on its community. To satisfy the economic impact requirement, the project being financed must do at least one of the following:

1. Create or retain jobs (one job per every $35,000 borrowed under SBA 504 (LIDC 2002).

OR

2. Accomplish one of the following public-policy goals:
   • Help revitalize a blighted community with a written revitalization plan,
   • Expand exports,
   • Promote minority businesses (owned 51 percent or more by a minority person),
   • Facilitate community or business change necessitated by federal budget cutbacks,
   • Accomplish change mandated by health, safety, or environmental standards, or
   • Increase productivity and competitiveness (retooling, robotics, and modernization).

OR

3. Achieve one of the following broad community-development goals:
   • Improve, diversify, or stabilize the local economy,
   • Stimulate other business development in the community,
   • Bring new income into the community,
   • Assist manufacturing firms, or
   • Assist businesses in a labor-surplus area.

Local CDCs can add requirements to satisfy local community needs (US SBA 2002).

Senior Lender. The loan made by the 504 corporation is to be a second-position loan. Therefore an applicant must bring proof to the application process that a bank or approved lending institution is willing to make a first mortgage under the rules of the program. A lender must express willingness to give a loan for about 50 percent of the purchase amount, and must extend the loan for at least one-half the length of term offered by the CDC loan. If no bank or approved non-bank lender is willing to make such a commitment, the loan is likely to be flawed and cannot go forward.

The first lender requirement, therefore, acts as a check on the judgment of the CDC.

CDC Loan and Downpayment. If a bank is willing to commit, the CDC then makes its own decision about the quality of the loan. If the loan appears both safe and beneficial to the community in terms of job creation, the CDC can preliminarily offer a second-position loan of up to 40 percent of the project cost, pending U.S. SBA approval. The small business must typically bring 10 percent to the table. The small business's equity commitment to the project rises to 15 percent if the financing is for limited-use assets and could rise to 20 percent if the business is a start-up. The CDC or some other financier could loan the business the downpayment as a third mortgage, but the CDC can only extend such loans with their own money. The SBA will not guarantee a subordinated debenture for such purposes.

Use of Proceeds. Applicants must have a defined real estate project or long-life equipment purchase that will act as the primary collateral for the loan. Specifically, funds may be used for any of the following:

- acquisition, construction, renovation or expansion of real estate;
- site improvements, including grading, streets, parking lots, utilities, or landscaping;
- leasehold improvements, and a small amount of furniture and fixtures;
- purchase and installation of machinery and equipment (including a vehicle or boat);
- interest on interim financing;
- points on project-related bridge loans;
- professional fees directly attributable and essential to the project including surveying, engineering, architectural or legal services, environmental reports, and permits;
- other associated soft costs such as title searches, title insurance, and appraisals.

Uses of 504 funds that are not permitted include mortgage broker fees, points on permanent financing, and moving expenses. Refinancing of old loans is not permitted except to take out financing on property acquired within the last nine months with interim funds. This exception to the rule is to facilitate property acquisition specifically related to the project.

Occupancy. The purpose of the program is not to promote real-estate speculation or real-estate development as a business. The purpose is to promote small business development and community development by improving business financial and locational stability. The real-estate aspect of the program accomplishes program goals by providing owner occupancy for small businesses.

The project being financed by a 504 loan package is to be occupied by the small business, not built for speculation. Yet, forcing businesses to build space only they would immediately occupy would be self-defeating. Such a policy would allow no space for growth of a successful business. Therefore, some excess space may be financed under the 504 program to facilitate future business expansion. The excess space can also be rented in the interim. Revenues from renting the space are counted as a part of the business' cash flow.

So, owners do not have to occupy 100 percent of the project facility. Owner-users of the 504-financed project must maintain 51 percent occupancy if the project rehabilitates an existing building. Sixty percent occupancy is required if new construction is involved. Two or more unrelated small businesses may receive a 504 loan to buy or construct a building in partnership as long as they, together, will occupy at least 51 percent of an existing building or 60 percent of new construction.

Source of Program Funds. The bank making the first-position mortgage must make the loan from its own funds without governmental assistance. If U.S. SBA approves, the money for the second-position loan is legally made by the CDC. The money to make the loan is supplied to the CDC by a complicated secondary-market process. The CDC is authorized to sell a debenture [historically to the Federal Finance Bank (FFB)].

Once each month the Development Company Finance Corporation with authorization from the federal government acts as fiscal agent to buy and bundle debentures from approximately 300 CDCs all over the country and sell the bundle as a bond to the general investing public. The bonds are marketable because the SBA guarantees 100 percent of value of the CDC debentures. The buyers of the bonds know that the U.S. government backs the bonds. As a result, the bonds sell at an interest rate moderately over that of comparable U.S. Treasury bonds. In a sense the U.S. government is facilitating a secondary market for CDC-secured and -guaranteed loans.

Private investors looking for fixed-income streams guaranteed by the federal government find this investment attractive. Examples of private investors include pension funds, life insurance companies, large banks, and individuals, under certain circumstances. The source of program funding is therefore primarily private. The Federal Government is a guarantor and facilitator only. The source of loan funds under the SBA 504 Loan Program is important to the program's existence. Most programs requiring continuing Federal subsidy do not enjoy longevity and suffer budgetary risks. Given that the source of funding for the 504 program is private and that the program participants reimburse any Federal subsidy, Congress has had little difficulty supporting this economic development program.

Typically the small business must make a downpayment of the remaining ten percent of the project cost. This equity contribution by the business often increases to 15 percent for a start-up company or for a project involving a unique building. However, the CDC may approve a third-position loan for any portion of the remaining percent with its own funds. Neither the SBA nor the DCFC will assist with this amount, and the loan must be subordinated to both the bank loan and the 504 loan.

Loan Size. The maximum debenture that a CDC can sell for a single deal is $1,000,000 ($1.3 million in certain situati ons). The minimum varies by CDC but is no less than $50,000 since that is the smallest debenture that the DCFC will handle and the SBA will guarantee (Dakota 2002; LIDC 2002; NADCO 2002).

Collateral and Security. The borrower must provide collateral to secure the loan. This may include a mortgage on the land and building being financed; liens on machinery, equipment and fixtures; lease agreements, and personal guarantees from individuals with 20 percent or greater ownership in the company (or limited guarantees from those with less than 20 percent ownership). The participating bank receives the first lien on the collateral; the CDC holds the second lien. Keyman life insurance is often required, particularly if there is no succession of management (LIDC 2002). Assignment of other assets of the business or principals is sometimes required, particularly if the company is a startup or the credit is unusually risky or the asset being financed is considered a single-purpose asset or doesn't appraise high enough (LIDC 2002).

Maturity. The 504 Program offers terms of ten years for loans that finance machinery and equipment and twenty years for real estate loans. The bank loan must have a term of at least half of the term offered on the second-position loan. This provision tends to stretch the loan length for small business loans from banks.

Interest and Servicing Fees. By buying CDC debentures, the DCFC supplies the funds to the local CDC at a rate approximately two percent over current rates of U.S. Treasury bonds of the same term. The CDC then makes the loan to the small business at that same rate plus servicing fees. The final interest rate charged to the business is determined at the time the 504 loan is funded based on going rates.

Alter-Ego Arrangements. Alter-ego arrangements are allowed under SBA 504. A primary financial advantage of owning real estate or long-life equipment is the ability to depreciate them. This non-cash accounting expense allows one to declare an accounting loss on paper. For sole proprietors and partners, paper losses may be passed through to a person's individual income-tax calculations, thus reducing taxable income and tax burden in many cases. Corporations may not pass paper losses to shareholders. If the borrowing business is a closely held corporation, for example, the corporation can gain little tax benefit from owning real estate. Individuals in many companies own the real estate through partnerships or sole proprietorships and then lease the real estate to their own corporation. This allows the real estate holder to depreciate the real-estate improvements, and pass any resulting paper losses on to their individual tax returns, while facilitating their company's operations.

A related issue is liability. The operating corporation faces most of the product or malpractice liability. The limited liability facilitated by the corporate structure argues for using the corporate organizational structure for the operating business. An alter-ego arrangement, where real estate is owned by a partnership of the principals of a corporation and the operating business is carried out by the corporation, provides the best of both worlds in terms of tax advantages and liability protection.

The SBA 504 program allows CDC loans to be made to the alter-ego partnership for the purchase of real estate and long-life equipment. For this to be allowed, (1) the percentage ownership of the partnership must match that of the closely held corporation, and (2) the items purchased with the loan must be used by that corporation to carry out the approved business activity.

Repayment and Prepayment. Loan repayment begins on the first day of the month following the sale of debentures. A prepayment penalty applies during the first half of the loan term, starting at 10 percent and declining to zero at the midlife of the loan (Dakota 2002) (LIDC 2002).

Interim Financing. Funding of the 504 portion of the loan package usually takes place within two months after the project is completed. This means that interim financing is required, usually by the local financial institution that holds the first mortgage or lien. The banker advances capital as the project begins and is repaid from or taken out by the proceeds of the SBA debenture.

The 504 corporation is a permanent lender only. It does not engage in construction or bridge financing unless it does so with its own funds. This means that, in most cases, the 50 percent-first mortgage lender (or someone else) will have to bridge the 504-loan portion until the project is complete (LIDC 2002).

The 504 corporation sells its bond and funds the loan when the certificate of occupancy is issued. Interest and fees on the bridge loan can be included in the project costs to be financed by the loan package. In New York the CDC can make the bridge loan exempt from NYS mortgage tax (LIDC 2002).

Principals (Owners). Owners must be U.S. citizens or registered aliens with a green card. Owners cannot be convicted felons currently on probation. Anyone who owns 20 percent or more of the operating company may be required to personally guarantee (unsecured general guarantee) the loan. Liquid assets of the owners are taken into account in determining eligibility. Too much liquid assets owned by a principal could disqualify the loan. The U.S. SBA might deem that the entrepreneurs could finance the project without SBA 504 assistance. At the least, SBA will require that all available assets will be pledged as collateral before approving a loan guarantee.

Fees. The 504 program requires payment of a one-time (processing) fee of approximately three percent of the CDC/SBA guaranteed portion of the loan package. About 1.5 percent goes to the CDC as a processing fee; one-half of one percent of the CDC loan is a reserve deposit; one-fourth of one percent is a loan-loss coverage fee. The remainder covers a guaranty fee, a funding fee and underwriting fees. It is important to note that the Federal subsidy for the guaranty is underwritten and funded by fees charged to the Program's participants rather than the Federal government.

Most likely, closing will cost $500 to $2700 including fees for title insurance and recording, and a legal fee. The participating bank pays an up-front fee of one-half of one percent of its loan to the CDC, which transfers the payment to the SBA (Dakota 2002).

All of the processing fees on the SBA 504 loan and some of the closing costs may be added to the loan amount so that the borrower can amortize their cost over the loan term. The borrower signs a note with the CDC for the 40 percent of project cost plus the fees.

After the loan closes, the monthly payment will include servicing fees based on the declining balance of the SBA 504 loan: seven-eighths percent to the CDC; one-eighth percent to SBA; one-tenth of one percent to a central servicing agent, usually a national bank that works for the SBA. Servicing fees are in addition to the one-time processing fees described above.

Payments. Payments on the SBA 504 loan are made by ACH debit from the borrower's designated checking account on the first of each month after the loan closes. Payments on the 504 loan are separate from pay-

Table 4.8
Typical 504 Financing Package

TYPICAL PROJECT EXAMPLE: $1,000,000 Real Estate Project			
Item	Bank	CDC	SBC
Loan Amount	$500,000	$400,000	$100,000
% of Project	50%	40%	10%
Interest Rate	pegged	fixed	equity
Maturity	10yrs.	20yrs.	n/a
Amortization	20 yr.	20 yr.	n/a
Interest Rate	Market	Fixed	n/a
Lien	First mortgage	Second mortgage	n/a

ments on the 50 percent first-mortgage loan, which are handled directly with the bank.

Table 4.8 illustrates a typical 504 loan package using simple numbers. Listed below are some typical deals financed by SBA 504.

- Distributor of horseradish, soups, mustard moved from Brooklyn to Long Island to buy a 75,000 square-foot warehouse to house its manufacturing, bottling, and distribution operations.
- An auto dealer custom built a new sales, repair, office complex.
- A CDC 504 provided funds to build the building and landscape for an all-weather two-tier driving range. The land was rented.
- A used commercial fishing vessel was purchased with CDC 504-provided funds.
- A CDC 504 provided the funds to construct a paddle-wheeler boat that cruises up and down a river providing breakfast, lunch, and dinner cruises.
- A dentist moved from inadequate rented space to a condominium office unit.
- A group of doctors built a state-of-the-art rehabilitation facility using CDC 504 funds.
- A printer bought two new 6-color printing presses.

- A machine shop renovated its building and bought equipment with CDC 504 funds.

- A mailing house expanded its building with a CDC 504 loan.

- A mattress discount business built a new warehouse and headquarters with CDC 504 financing.

- An accountant bought and renovated a building to house his offices with CDC/SBA 504 funding (LIDC 2002).

Evaluation of the CDC 504 Program

Business Borrower Perspective

The Certified Development Corporation program provides some relief from many of the problems associated with typical bank small business financing, while, at the same time, involving banks in the process. It offers fixed-interest-rate financing that avoids variable interest fluctuations. The program offers low down payments (10 percent compared with a more typical 30 percent for bank financing), and a longer term than typically available to small businesses. The provision that forces the first mortgage lender to provide a term that is at least half the CDC-loan term tends to stretch the bank loan to ten years on real estate, compared with a more typical three to five years. These advantages stabilize monthly debt service and help to reduce monthly payment levels to be in line with cash-flow requirements.

The loan analysis on the CDC portion of the loan carried out by both CDC staff and SBA loan officers is, in most cases, more cash-flow oriented and less collateral oriented than the typical banker analysis of a small business loan. This might not make receiving the loan any easier for the business. On the contrary, shining a different light on the business' operations might make receiving the loan package more difficult. Yet, this might be a beneficial protection for the business. Being collateral oriented, banks sometimes feel safe offering loans that have excellent collateral coverage without sufficient scrutiny to the assumptions that underlie the pro forma. In the process, a small business with a weak business plan might be induced to go into deeper debt than it can handle, At the same time it might overcollateralize the loan, putting too many business and personal assets at risk.

The CDC program is designed to provide financing for real estate and long-life equipment only. Some would claim that the purpose of this rule is not to induce businesses to own more fixed assets. Rather, it is part of a mechanism to induce traditional lenders to take on midrisk situations. It is a way to channel debt capital to small businesses that could not otherwise receive financing since banks are able to make loans with solid collateral and a low loan-to-value ratio.

Some would claim that the real benefit to businesses is improvement to their cash flow, not just fixed-asset ownership. With such a loan they, in effect, amortize the rent that they would otherwise have to pay. With a low down payment they create a situation in which their monthly payments are less than equivalent rents. Many CDCs sell the program to small businesses not based on some need to buy real estate, but as a way to improve cash flow.

A critical question is, what effect does the program have on business behavior? For example, does the program induce businesses to go too deeply into debt before businesses are ready? At what level are the business' principals ready emotionally, financially, intellectually, and otherwise to take out a loan? What do banks and the SBA look at in a loan application? Banks are collateral lenders. A second-position 504 CDC loan will induce banks to lend more freely.

Who is helping the small business decide on the appropriate level and timing of debt? Some certified development corporations are tied into the local system of enterprise development, but many are not. No research has been conducted to determine if businesses receiving 504 loans have been more or less successful, or if so, why?

Senior Lender Perspective

A bank wishing to participate as the 50 percent first-mortgage lender experiences several benefits. The lender gets Community Reinvestment Act credits. The bank is able to lend at a lower loan-to-value ratio and has lower risk than it would with a conventional loan because the SBA 504 loan is in second position behind the bank. Since the CDC loan is a subordinated loan, the CDC's ability to pay off the debenture and therefore the SBA's guarantee of the debenture are most at risk if the loan becomes non performing. The federal government shares much of the loan's risk through the SBA's debenture guarantee. CDCs experience some risk in that they are responsible to ensure that information provided to the SBA is correct.

Banks may also be able to sell the first mortgage in the secondary mortgage market. Other advantages to the primary lender of participation in the 504 program include liquidity management, managing overall lending limits, and strengthening core earnings through a highly marketable commercial-lending product (Wallace 2001). Advantages of the program that should not be overlooked are that the program also allows a bank to keep a growing customer happy, and promotes the economic development of the bank's home community.

What effect the reduction in bank risk has had on bank behavior is not known. Have banks offered more loans than they otherwise would have? If so, how many? Have the borrowing businesses and, therefore, their loans been more successful? Anecdotal evidence says yes, to both questions, but no systematic independent evaluation has confirmed the effect of the 504 CDC program on bank, CDC or SBC behavior, and the quantity of the effect has never been determined.

Community Perspective

The community receives the advantage of keeping or attracting a healthy, growing small business that creates jobs and promotes community improvement. The stated and probable advantages of the 504 program to the community are job creation and broader economic development.

Job Creation. The U.S. SBA literature and Web site claim that the SBA's 504 program has approved more than 54,000 loans; provided more than $19 billion in guaranteed debentures (NADCO 2002); and assisted in the creation of more than 4.4 million jobs since the program began in 1987. It is claimed that more than 4.4 million jobs were also retained (Hook 2002). This does not count its predecessor 503 program that initiated certified development corporations in 1983. Based on a crude calculation of the ratio, the creation of one job requires about $4,300 in SBA-guaranteed debentures. But, these numbers are based on CDC self-reporting and are expected to be highly inflated. The numbers are the compilation of only a crude estimate entered onto a loan application form. Moreover, no independent, objective analysis indicates the degree to which jobs created are new, or ones displace from somewhere else. No independent researcher has completed a follow-up to see how many jobs continued after six month or two years. The SBA is mandated to follow-up the job-creation estimates two years after the loan, but it does not visit all job sites.

Economic Development. Even more vague and uncertain is the stated accomplishment of other goals of the program. Some of those goals include:

- Improving, diversifying, or stabilizing the local economy
- Stimulating other business development in the community

- Bringing new income into the community
- Assisting manufacturing firms
- Assisting businesses in a labor-surplus area.
- Helping to revitalize a blighted community with a written revitalization plan
- Expansion of exports
- Developing minority business (owned 51 percent or more by minority business person)
- Increasing productivity and competitiveness (retooling, robotics, modernization) (U.S. SBA 2002).

No report summarizes what percentage of businesses receiving loans claim to have promoted the accomplishment of these objectives.

Cost to Government. Theoretically, the money for the program comes from private investors because the bundle of debentures is sold to private investors. SBA also claims that administrative costs and the government's loan-guarantee expenses are covered by the service fee structure. No independent audits confirm these notions, but it is clear that the program is fairly low cost. Some of the administrative costs are carried by the local CDCs. Many nonprofit CDCs have volunteer board members and attorneys.

Perfection of Markets. One evaluative issue related to government intervention in the financial markets is whether the program improves the workings of free markets or distorts markets. Three markets to discuss are the financial intermediaries, the real estate markets, and other business markets.

Does the program distort or perfect *money markets* and affect the workings of financial intermediaries? It seems apparent that the 504 program is helping the problem of small business financing. Probably, more money is flowing to small business than otherwise would, but no rigorous research has shown the effect of the program on bank behavior. The only thing we know is that bank risk is reduced by the program and banks are giving first position loans under the rules of the program, but we do not know how many of those loans would have been made conventionally without the program. Banks are also providing longer-term loans than normal because of the program.

One might assume that since the program requires the purchase of real estate or long-life equipment, it pulls money toward facilities and long-life equipment. Some might claim that this distorts money markets, causing communities to overbuild commercial and industrial facilities. Maybe lack of physical capital is not the problem the economy faces. Others would claim that the fixed-capital emphasis is really just a way to stabilize business finances and, because of the low down payment and longer term, improve small business cash flow. The idea of pursuing a 504 loan is often sold to a small business based on the cash-flow argument.

What does the program do to *real estate markets?* Does the emphasis on owner occupancy stabilize neighborhoods and communities by creating businesses that are more stable locationally and financially? Or, does having so much of a business's assets tied up in real estate decrease business flexibility, innovation, and mobility? No studies have addressed these issues. Is promotion of small business ownership of real estate a good thing? Since the program promotes new development, one question is whether we need more physical facilities for commercial and industrial activities. We do not know what percentage of the projects financed are new as opposed to revitalized. Does the emphasis on physical development cause more sprawl rather than help businesses in disadvantaged areas? We know that the program offers a very slight incentive to revitalize older space since the mandated occupancy percentage is lower for revitalization. We do not know what percent of the funded projects are in declining areas versus greenfields.

One study by Daniel Immergluck and Erin Mullen of 504 loan activity in the metropolitan Chicago area addressed some of these questions. They concluded that, after controlling for firm density, firm size, and industrial mix, higher-income areas and outlying zip codes receive more loans than did lower-income and closer-in areas (Immergluck and Mullen 1998). In other words, 504 loans might be contributing more to sprawl than to inner-city redevelopment. Although the study does not conclude this, the program might even be inducing firms to leave inner cities and move to greenfield sites by offering them an attractive financial package to move to a new owner-occupied facility. Immergluck and Mullen do not claim that inner-city businesses are being denied loans consciously. Rather, they suggest that a variety of natural supply-side and demand-side forces affect both bank participation and 504-marketing activity differently in different parts of the metropolitan area in much the same way that they do any lending activity. Their study reinforces the point that if a government program wants to benefit disadvantaged areas, targeting mechanisms must be built into the program. Then, the question is, how much targeting can be achieved before beneficial natural-market forces are destroyed?

Does the program add to the number of *companies* in over-supplied business areas such as pizza places, dentists, car dealers, and liquor stores? The federal government provides no breakdown of financing by SIC code.

Summary

Government can perfect money markets and induce debt capital to flow to midrisk situations by participating in a subordinated loan program. By allowing traditional lending institutions to make first-position loans with low loan-to-value ratios supported by subordinated loans, banks are more willing to lend to small businesses. The governmental involvement leverages the private bank financing.

The Certified Development Corporation is a national program in the U.S. authorized under the U.S. Small Business Act. The program certifies local development corporations (CDCs) to make subordinated loans and sell federally guaranteed debentures to a central fiscal agent to fund the loans. The debenture purchaser then packages the debentures and sells them as bonds.

The bank, the U.S. Small Business Administration and the business that makes a down payment share risk. The local CDC and the buyer of the federally backed bonds share a small amount of risk. The bank makes loans at a lower risk then conventional loans. The business receives a loan with longer maturity and lower interest. The community experiences economic development.

While the program works well mechanically and seems to induce the desired bank behavior, no objective, independent research has confirmed this fact. Anecdotally, the program also seems to promote business success. Yet several questions remain to be answered. Are businesses induced to borrow the right amount at the right time? Are entrepreneurs ready to take on the debt provided?

Also unclear is the effect of a fixed-asset program on businesses. Is owning real estate appropriate for young, small businesses? Does it create inflexibility and overemphasis on capital-intensive business practices? Is the fixed-asset approach assisting disadvantaged communities or inducing sprawl? Is the program creating success in businesses that truly diversify the community's economic base or just producing an oversupply of some service businesses? Independent analysis is necessary to answer these questions.

SHORTCOMINGS OF CURRENT PRACTICES

Each of the tools for debt-capital formation discussed above possesses certain advantages and each has a role to play in fostering small business activity in the United States. However, individually, and when taken together, these capital provision vehicles have several major shortcomings that limit their effectiveness in the long run.

First, these sources of debt capital tend to be fragmented and categorical (Lyons 2002). They often operate in isolation of each other, even in a single locality or region. There is typically little or no interaction among them. Each has its own culture and jargon and, in some cases, is represented by its own professional association. This tends to highlight the differences and widen the gap between them.

This fragmentation also causes them to operate in a nonsystemic way. They are opaque to the entrepreneurs they seek to serve. It is unclear what role each plays and at what stage of a company's development a particular debt-capital provider can be most helpful. It is left to the entrepreneur to sort these things out for him- or herself. This results in confusion, with entrepreneurs attempting to enter the debt-capital provision "system" at inappropriate places, being turned away, and left to wonder why. This can be a bewildering and discouraging experience—one that reduces the ranks of entrepreneurs rather than expands them.

Fragmentation also makes for inefficient service delivery. Too often, there is either a gap in debt-capital provision or unproductive overlap within a particular economic region. Because providers are often unaware of what each other is doing and entrepreneurs have an unclear picture as well, no one can see the gaps or the overlap.

Second, debt-capital providers have tended to make unilateral decisions about the services they provide before they understand the needs of the small business owners that they seek to serve. The underutilization of micro-loan monies is an excellent example of this problem. Had micro-lenders not merely adopted the Grameen Bank model in a more-or-less "cookie cutter" fashion, and, instead, determined what low-income entrepreneurs in the United States actually need and want, they may have been able to avoid the decline in the demand for micro-loans. Only recently have they been able to determine the reasons for this problem by talking to micro-entrepreneurs and to take corrective action. Similarly, capital access programs do not have a primary focus of developing entrepreneurs. They are vehicles that banks can use to plug collateral holes of not-quite bankable companies. While CAPs do address certain entrepreneurial needs, they do so in a somewhat backhanded fashion.

This lack of attention to the needs of client entrepreneurs tends to obscure the fact that debt capital is merely a resource. Simply providing it, or providing it at reduced cost, does not ensure that the entrepreneur can utilize it effectively, nor does it teach the entrepreneur how to avoid future capital problems. To borrow an old metaphor, it "gives the entrepreneur a fish, but does not necessarily teach her/him how to fish." This is because, with the possible exception of some comprehensive microenterprise programs, the provision of debt capital involves short-term, arms-length, transactional relationships. Such relationships, by themselves, are incapable of effecting the kind of transformation necessary to fully develop an entrepreneur (Lyons 2002). Transformation involves qualitative changes on many levels over time (Lichtenstein and Lyons 2001). Debt-capital provision can play a role in such a transformation, if it is done well. However, this suggests that it must be focused on the development of the entrepreneur, not on the business and certainly not on the capital provider, itself.

Third, many debt-capital providers labor under evaluation and record-keeping deficiencies. As was discussed relative to BIDCOs and CDCs, in particular, no independent assessments of their impacts, or of their value to entrepreneurs, have been conducted. This makes it difficult, if not impossible, to know whether or not government investment in these programs is providing a suitable return to taxpayers. What information providers collect is inadequate and inconsistent across provider organizations. Uniform data-collection policies and procedures, and a uniform database, would greatly help this situation (Lyons 2001).

Finally, individual capital providers often see themselves in competition with other lenders in their region for a fixed number of client entrepreneurs (Lichtenstein and Lyons 2001). This kind of competition is unnecessary and unproductive for two reasons:

- There is not a limited supply of prospective entrepreneurs. This is a myth perpetuated by a stubborn adherence to the notion that successful entrepreneurs possess certain innate traits when, in fact, successful entrepreneurship is based in the possession and mastery of a skill set (Shefsky 1996; Lichtenstein and Lyons 2001). This latter view expands the pool of prospective entrepreneurs and removes the limitations imposed by an assumption of a fixed supply.

- Different capital providers operate at different levels. They work with entrepreneurs whose skill levels are compatible with their capacity to assist those entrepreneurs. Furthermore, they work with companies that are at a specific stage(s) of their evolution (Lichtenstein and Lyons 2001). Thus, if each provider is playing its appropriate role, there is no need for intra-regional competition.

This latter observation suggests a hierarchy of capital provision. While capital providers may implicitly understand this hierarchy, it has not been made explicit. If it was to become explicit, this would go a long way toward making capital provision more transparent to entrepreneurs and helping capital providers to understand their roles vis-à-vis each other. In turn, this would enhance the capital provision community's ability to function in a more systemic fashion, heightening its ability to transform entrepreneurs and the regional economy.

REFERENCES

Avery, R. B., R. W. Bostic, and K. A. Samolyk, 1998. The Role of Personal Wealth in Small Business Finance. August 22, 6–8: 1019–1061 (43).

Berger, A. N., and G. F. Udel. 1995. Relationship Lending and Lines of Credit in Small Firm Finance. *Journal of Business.* 68: 351–382.

CCH. 2002. Business Owners Toolkit: Total Know-how for Small Businesses. http://www.toolkit.cch.com/text/P10 4240.asp. (July 18).

Czarnecki, J. 2002. Vice President, Community Services, Michigan Economic Development Corporation. Interviewed. April 13.

Dakota Certified Development Corporation. 2002. http://www.dakotacdc.com/loan/index.html. (July 10).

Enchantment Land Certified Development Corporation. 2002. (http://www.elcdc.com/) (June 15).

Hamlin, R. E. 1998. *The Capital Access Program: An Evaluation of Economic Benefit.* Lansing, MI: The Michigan Jobs Commission.

Hamlin, R. E. 1999. Capital Access Programs Spur Growth. Urban Policy Briefing No. 99–2. Program in Politics and Policy, Michigan State University.

Hamlin, R. E., and Florin Sabastian Duma. 1999. The Capital Access Program: Its Application for Eastern Europe. *European Traditions and Experiences.* Ladislau Gyemant, (ed.) Cluj-Napoca: European Studies Foundation Publishing House.

Hamlin, R. E. 2002. Public-Private Partnership for Inner-city Redevelopment. In C. S. Weissert, D. W. Thornton, and A. M. Schneider. *Urban Policy Options for Michigan Leaders,* eds. East Lansing: Michigan State University Press.

Hayes, G. W. 1993. A Comparison of Borrowers with SBA and Other Loan Guarantees. Unpublished dissertation. Montana State University.

Hook, D. 2002. Chief, Finance Division, Michigan District Office, U.S. Small Business Administation. E-mail. July 9.

Immergluck, D., and E. Mullen 1998. The Intrametropolitan Distribution of Economic Development Financing: An Analysis of SBA 504 Lending Patterns. *Economic Development Quarterly,* November.

Lichtenstein, G. A., and T. S. Lyons. 1996. *Incubating New Enterprises: A Guide to Successful Practice.* Washington, D.C.: The Aspen Institute.

Lichtenstein, G. A., and T. S. Lyons. 2001. The Entrepreneurial Development System: Transforming Business Talent and Community Economies. *Economic Development Quarterly* 15, 1:3–20.

Lyons, T. S. 2002. *The Entrepreneurial League System®: Transforming Your Community's Economy through Enterprise Development.* Washington, D.C.: The Appalachian Regional Commission.

Lyons, T. S. 2001. *Articulating the Current Minority Business Development System in Louisville, Kentucky.* Louisville: Center for Research on Entrepreneurship and Enterprise Development, College of Business and Public Administration, University of Louisville.

Long Island Development Corporation (LIDC). 2002. www.lidc.org. (July 3)

McKinney, Kathline. 2002. Business Bucks: Government Programs Open Lenders Door, Indiana Business Magazine, January

Michigan Jobs Commission. 1996. *Capital Access Program* (Informational Report).

NADCO, the National Association of Development Companies. 2002. http://nadco.org (July 3).

Osborne, D. E., and P. Plasterik. 1997. Backing the Unbankable. *The Washington Post.* Sunday, September 14; W07.

Oliver, M. L., and T. M. Shapiro. 1995. *Black Wealth/White Wealth.* Boston: Routledge Kegan Paul.

Sandstedt, S. 2002. President of Capitol BIDCO, President of Priority Development, and owner of Lenco Products. Interviewed, July 3.

Shefsky, L. E. 1996. *Entrepreneurs Are Made Not Born.* New York: McGraw-Hill.

U.S. Small Business Administration. 2002. www.sba.gov/financing (July 3)

U.S. Treasury, Department of. 1998. *The Capital Access Program: A Summary of Nationwide Performance.* Treasury Report No.3102. Washington, D.C.: October 15.

U.S. Treasury, Department of. 2001. The Capital Access Program: A Summary of Nationwide Performance. Washington, D.C.: January.

Wallace, T. 2001. SBA 504 Loans: An Underused Program that Helps Community Banks. *The RMA Journal.* Philadelphia: April.

Chapter 5

SUMMARY AND CONCLUSION

SUMMARY

Small businesses have played, and will continue to play, a major role in the U.S. economy. Among some of the best-known corporations in America are many that started out as an entrepreneur, or entrepreneurial team, with an idea, including Dell Computers, Federal Express, Mary Kay Cosmetics, and Starbucks Coffee, to name only a few. Small businesses employ a significant portion of our workforce and continue to create the majority of new jobs. They are sources of innovation. They are suppliers to large corporations. Small firms have helped to assimilate immigrants into the U.S. economy and culture, and they have provided an avenue to economic progress for women and minorities.

The globalization of the economy has brought with it major structural changes as well as changes in the rules of the economic game. These changes have produced important challenges to the survival, let alone success, of small businesses. They must now contend with an economy in which they must actively recruit and retain high-level human capital. They must cope with a highly diversified economic system as well as an equally diverse array of specialized business resources. They must seek out and capture global niche markets. They must develop strategic alliances and frequently reinvent themselves if they are to survive.

Because of the tremendous value that small businesses add to the U.S. economy, helping them to overcome the challenges of the global economy is in the public interest. This means that it makes sense for government agencies and quasi-governmental entities to intervene in markets to foster small business success.

This intervention can take a variety of forms. It may involve providing technical and business management training. Making connections between and among small businesses to encourage strategic alliances is another way in which governments can intervene in a useful manner. Yet another form of intervention is the provision of debt capital, which has been the focus of this book. Intervention in debt capital markets also comes in a variety of forms. Governments may intervene directly. They may provide debt capital through quasi-public entities. They might also stimulate debt-capital provision through private institutions, such as banks.

In order for capital markets to work effectively, a balance must be achieved between the perceived risk and perceived rewards faced by a variety of types of investors. Capital markets are flawed in that the middle range of the risk/reward spectrum, between conventional bank lending and venture capital, does not work well. This is exactly the segment of the capital markets that is most important to small businesses. Government can improve the flow of middle-risk, debt capital by sanctioning institutions and sharing risk in the middle-risk realm in much the way it does with conventional, lower-risk debt markets. As with all governmental interventions, it should be done with caution and with sensitivity to natural market forces. Otherwise, undesirable market dislocations and feedback will result. One should take care to develop strong institutions and promote participation by current debt capitalists where possible, rather than crowd out existing private actors.

The tools of middle-risk debt capital provision tend to fall into two major categories: direct assistance to relatively higher-risk situations and indirect incentives to help "almost bankable" situations. Relatively higher-risk debt-capital provision is targeted at nascent entrepreneurs who lack the skills, experience, and resources to attract private capital. Their businesses are typically, young, untested, and in industries that are not perceived as being high growth. Yet, they have a valuable role to play in the local economy. This kind of debt-capital provision requires the government to lend directly to these small businesses, either through micro-lending programs or revolving loan funds. Therein lies the higher level of risk, as discussed in Chapter 3.

Indirect approaches to medium-risk debt capital discussed in Chapter 4 are aimed at encouraging lending to entrepreneurs who are not quite bankable. That is, their skills, experience and resources are greater than those of the higher-risk entrepreneurs, but they still do not quite meet the expectations and requirements of private, conventional lending institutions. Nevertheless, they are close enough that it is possible for government to intervene through loan guarantees, loan insurance pooling, loans with equity kickers and subordinated lending to encourage private lending to these small businesses. These tools allow government to share the risk, thereby reducing it for all concerned.

As was discussed in Chapters 3 and 4, the tools for delivering medium-risk debt capital have their distinct advantages and disadvantages. Chief among the advantages is their ability to improve the functioning of debt capital markets and make debt capital available in situations where the free market does not otherwise provide it. This makes for more efficient and equitable delivery of debt capital to an important component of the economy.

While the advantages are important and provide a sound basis for success in this arena, the shortcomings are disturbing because they stand as barriers to achievement of the capital delivery system's full potential. These shortcomings include the following:

- The debt capital sources are fragmented and categorical;
- Fragmentation causes them to operate in a nonsystemic way;
- Fragmentation makes for inefficient service delivery;
- Fragmentation makes the capital delivery "system" opaque to entrepreneurs;
- Debt-capital providers make decisions about what services they will offer without first determining what their prospective clients actually need;
- Debt-capital provision is largely transactional; not transformational;
- Program evaluation and record keeping is deficient among providers, creating an accountability vacuum; and
- Debt-capital providers, like service providers in all realms of entrepreneurship assistance, sincerely, yet incorrectly, see themselves as being in competition with each other.

When taken together, these deficiencies reflect an existing paradigm of capital provision that is outdated and in need of substantial renovation. Perhaps, it is now time to consider something new.

CONCLUSION

What is needed in the capital-provision arena is a systemic view of all capital-provision activities, a strategic approach to matching types of capital to individual entrepreneurs and small businesses that need it; and a systematic approach to delivering that capital. This would go a long way toward addressing the shortcomings outlined above.

Capital provision, both that made available by public or quasi-public organizations and that offered by private entities, is implicitly a system. It is a system with a distinct hierarchy, based upon the perception of risk surrounding the given entrepreneur or business. That perception of risk is grounded in several factors: the skill level of the entrepreneur or entrepreneurial team, the business's place in its own evolution, the perceived strength of the business concept, the characteristics of the entrepreneur (e.g.: low income, minority status, gender, etc.), and the location of the business.

This implicit hierarchy of capital provision might be thought of as a ladder, with different capital providers operating at different rungs (Lyons 2002). The bottom rung consists of the high-risk entrepreneurs who may be low-income and or minority individuals. They often have start-up businesses in industries that are viewed to be marginal. These businesses are often located in poor, inner-city neighborhoods or rural communities. The entrepreneurs, themselves, may be nascent; that is, they are completely new to owning and operating a business and have few skills in this regard. The capital providers who serve at this rung of the ladder are the microenterprise programs and revolving loan funds, that are government, or quasi-governmental, organizations designed specifically to assist this unserved market. Before these programs came along, this rung in the capital ladder was missing. This left a considerable number of entrepreneurs out of the capital provision system, as they were not able to make the leap to a higher rung of the ladder.

At the next rung of the ladder are the medium-risk, or almost bankable, entrepreneurs. It is at this level that the loan guarantee, loan insurance pooling, loans with equity kickers and subordinated lending programs operate. These, too, are governmental, or quasi-governmental interventions aimed at perfecting capital markets. They attempt to do so by inducing private lenders to take on these medium-risk entrepreneurs.

The third rung of the capital provision ladder is occupied by bankable businesses that need debt capital. Private lending institutions are the capital providers at this level. To this point, all of the forms of capital provided are debt capital and have been the subject of this book.

The remaining rungs of the ladder involve forms of equity capital. The fourth rung is angel capital. Angel capitalists are most commonly wealthy individuals, very frequently successful entrepreneurs, who seek to invest in growing businesses, in part to make money and in part as a way of "giving back." This semi-philanthropic purpose causes angel capitalists to require less control over the business in which they are investing and to exact a lower return on their investment than do venture capitalists, who operate at the fifth rung of the capital provision ladder. Venture capitalists provide much larger equity injections than do angels and are looking for much larger returns on their investments. They are taking the greatest risks of any capital provider on the ladder and, therefore, seek out the highest level entrepreneurs and businesses.

Depending upon where a given entrepreneur and her/his business stand relative to the risk factors itemized above, and upon their needs, that entrepreneur might enter the capital provision "system" at any level. However, most entrepreneurs are not ready to start out at the highest rungs of the ladder. For many, they and their businesses must undergo an evolutionary process before they are ready for angel or venture capital. That evolution may start all the way down at the lowest rung of the ladder, with a direct loan from a microenterprise program or a revolving loan fund. Once the entrepreneur demonstrates that he has mastered this initial form of debt capital, he can "step up" to one of the types of medium-risk debt capital. Upon demonstrating that he is bankable, the entrepreneur can pursue a private bank loan. By now, the entrepreneur has developed his skills and grown his business to a place where it may be attractive to an angel capitalist. Successful growth and development through angel capital may, then, attract the attention of a venture capitalist. In fact, increasingly, angel capital investment has become a pre-requisite to venture capital investment.

Unfortunately, as noted previously, this hierarchy of capital provision is not explicit and, therefore, not readily visible to entrepreneurs in need of capital. They tend to try to enter the "system" at improper places. When this happens, they are either rebuffed or, if screening mechanisms fail, placed in jeopardy at a rung on the ladder that is too high for them at the time. This problem is exacerbated by the other shortcomings of debt capital noted previously, in particular the fragmentation and the categorical nature of the providers and the fact that capital solutions are prescribed without a true diagnosis of needs of the entrepreneur and her business.

The solution to this problem may lie in the explicit creation of a capital provision system at the local or regional level. One that makes the ladder clear to entrepreneurs and that, through collaboration among providers, ensures that they can advance on the ladder in a manner that is appropriate to their needs. Such a system would require an initial assessment component that would identify the needs and the skill levels of entrepreneurs coming into the system. It also would need a mechanism for continued monitoring of entrepreneurs and their businesses to ensure progress. Finally, the system would require a uniform record keeping and accountability scheme to permit providers to work together successfully.

Lichtenstein and Lyons (2001) have developed a system designed to organize entrepreneurs by skill level and enterprise development service providers by their capacity to assist entrepreneurs at a given skill level. While it is beyond the scope of this book to describe it in detail, the Entrepreneurial Development System (EDS), as they call it, provides the kind of framework that would permit debt-capital providers to take their appropriate place in the enterprise development system of their locality or region. It affords a systemic, strategic, and systematic way to overcome the shortcomings of debt-capital provision practice described above. This makes it, at the very least, worthy of further exploration.

REFERENCES

Lichtenstein, G. A., and T. S. Lyons. 2001. "The Entrepreneurial Development System: Transforming Business Talent and Community Economies." *Economic Development Quarterly* 15, 1:3–20.

Lyons, T. S. 2002. The Entrepreneurial League System®: Transforming Your Community's Economy Through Enterprise Development. Washington, D.C.: Appalachian Regional Commission.

INDEX

About the Authors

ROGER E. HAMLIN is Professor of Urban and Regional Planning, Professor of Public Administration, and Research Fellow in the Institute for Public Policy and Social Research at Michigan State University. He and Thomas S. Lyons are coauthors of *Creating an Economic Development Action Plan: A Guide for Development Professionals, Revised and Updated Edition* (Praeger, 2001) and *Economy without Walls: Managing Local Development in a Restructuring World* (Praeger, 1996).

THOMAS S. LYONS is Associate Professor of Urban and Public Affairs, University of Louisville. He is the Director of the Master of Urban Planning Program and founding Director of the Center for Research on Entrepreneurship and Enterprise Development.